"Martin and Osterling describe why value stream mapping is necessary for *any* organization and how it can be used as the means to achieve strategic transformation. They've done a fabulous job at explaining the what, why, and how, as well as the pitfalls to avoid. Follow the guidelines in this book and watch your performance soar."

—Raju Deshpande, Senior Vice President,
East West Bank

"*Value Stream Mapping* is a wise and practical guide that will help you lead transformation efforts in your organization. While some think of value stream mapping as a 'Lean tool,' Martin and Osterling rightly emphasize the strategic value of looking at the big picture and improving your entire value stream from suppliers to the customer and all points in between. The book is full of tips and lessons learned to help you avoid mistakes and maximize the results that you get from the time invested into proper value stream mapping."

—Mark Graban, author, *Lean Hospitals*

"Value stream mapping has helped many organizations understand not only how to see, but to also improve and enhance the value they produce and deliver to their customers. But understanding how to accomplish this in information-intensive businesses has been a substantial gap in business and industry. Martin and Osterling unleash and deliver the principles, practices, and tools for organizations to not only fill this gap but, from their extensive hands-on experience, to understand, actuate, and extensively transform value streams to maximize enterprise-wide customer value."

—Jim Huntzinger, President & Founder,
Lean Frontiers, and author, *Lean Cost Management*

"Despite decades of viewing value stream mapping as the core tool of Lean transformations, there is still confusion. Karen and Mike put mapping in its proper perspective as a methodology for getting high-performing teams to see waste, share a future state vision, and build meaningful actions that are carried out with passion and purpose."

—Jeffrey Liker, author, *The Toyota Way*

"Value stream mapping stands as the best tool available to really grasp what's happening in your supply chain—allowing you to focus your improvement activities for maximum benefit. Nobody does a better job than Martin and Osterling of laying out the nuts and bolts of engaging all levels in your organization in the application of value stream mapping to feed high impact continuous improvement. This is one of the best books available on the subject—buy it, teach it, use it—and your supply chain will become a competitive weapon!"

—Kevin Limbach, Vice President, U.S. Operations,
TaylorMade-adidas Golf Company

"Martin and Osterling have written an excellent book that shows you how to do value stream mapping and do it right. Follow their advice and your organization will get the profoundly radical change required to better serve your customers and create unprecedented profits and agility."

—Brian Maskell, author, *Practical Lean Accounting*

"Building on past works, *Value Stream Mapping* goes beyond the tool itself and effectively describes the leadership practices required to identify, improve, and manage value streams. Of particular note is the discussion on sustaining improvements, which is often difficult or even ignored. Karen and Mike describe how appropriate leadership systems can make it surprisingly easy. Wide-ranging examples make this book valuable to any industry or function."

—Kevin Meyer, former President, Specialty Silicone
Fabricators, Inc., and author, *Evolving Excellence*

"Value stream mapping has evolved from its roots as a tool used by geeks to reimagine and reconfigure manufacturing operations to a process to enable deep organizational intervention and transformation. With *Value Stream Mapping*, Karen Martin and Mike Osterling provide an outstanding guide for practitioners engaged in the challenging work of improving the horizontal flow of value across organizations."

—John Shook, Chairman and CEO, Lean Enterprise
Institute, and coauthor, *Learning to See*

"This is more than a primer on value stream mapping. Martin and Osterling hone in on the key conditions that should be set in place to ensure a successful outcome, and how value stream mapping can better align the leadership team. These pearls of wisdom and insight come from their many years facilitating and deploying Lean in a wide range of organizations, companies, and institutions."

—Rick Sunamoto, Vice President, Manufacturing,
HM Electronics, Inc.

VALUE
STREAM
MAPPING

VALUE STREAM MAPPING

How to Visualize Work and Align Leadership for Organizational Transformation

Karen Martin
AND Mike Osterling

New York   Chicago   San Francisco   Athens   London   Madrid
Mexico City   Milan   New Delhi   Singapore   Sydney   Toronto

15   LCR   21

ISBN   978-0-07-182891-8
MHID 0-07-182891-5

e-ISBN   978-0-07-182894-9
e-MHID 0-07-182894-X

Library of Congress Cataloging-in-Publication Data
Martin, Karen.
  Value stream mapping : how to visualize work and align leadership for
organizational transformation / Karen Martin and Mike Osterling. —
1 Edition.
     pages cm
   ISBN 978-0-07-182891-8 (hardback) — ISBN 0-07-182891-5
   1. Organizational change. 2. Cost effectiveness. 3. Leadership.
I. Osterling, Mike. II. Title.
  HD58.8.M2867 2013
  658.4'034—dc23

                                        2013032407

McGraw-Hill Education books are available at special quantity discounts
to use as premiums and sales promotions or for use in corporate training
programs. To contact a representative, please visit the Contact Us pages at
www.mhprofessional.com.

FROM MIKE
To my wife, Dianne, and our sons, Ryan and Sean,
for their sacrifices and support on this journey.

Without their inspiration and patience this undertaking
would not have been possible.

FROM KAREN
To Jenna Martin, a natural Lean thinker and
a bundle of talent.

I appreciate deeply all that I continuously learn from this
inspiring and kindhearted young lady.

Contents

Acknowledgments

Very few people know how many times—and for how many years—we considered writing this book and then decided against it. We felt that the value stream mapping ship had sailed. But the more we talked with improvement professionals and leaders from a wide range of industries and learned of the struggles they encountered on their journey toward operational excellence, the more we realized that there was indeed a gap in the business book marketplace that needed to be filled. The true catalyst for writing this book, and sharing our perspective on value stream mapping, resulted from repeated requests from our peers, readers of our previous books, workshop and webinar participants, social media connections, and our own clients. Many people who had heard of or experimented with value stream mapping wanted to gain a deeper understanding than was available on the subject. So our first batch of thank yous (yes, we're batching) is for all of those people who asked, graciously accepted our reasons for not wanting to write this book, and then asked again. Without your encouragement and persistence, this book would likely not exist.

Our second batch of thank yous goes to Dan Jones, Beau Keyte, John Krafcik, Jeff Liker, Drew Locher, Daniel Roos, Mike Rother, John Shook, and Jim Womack. Each of these gentlemen is a trailblazer who has contributed to the transformation of businesses and industries around the world. Without their profound knowledge and thought leadership, we would likely still be wrestling with how best to help organizations design effective and efficient operations, connect more deeply with their customers, learn to see the truth about their performance, and ease the process of improvement and organizational transformation. Without these great minds and their insights, we would have neither the client experiences nor the knowledge required to attempt an undertaking such as this book.

Thank you, too, to the crackerjack team at iGrafx—especially Kim Scott and Gretchen Burthey—who generously gave their time, expertise, and development skills to find the best way to present the value stream maps in a format that works for both print and e-books. Your responsiveness and patience was a godsend.

Heartfelt thank yous go to our friends and colleagues who gave their time to read the book, gave constructive feedback, and offered kind words when warranted: Steve Bell, Ed Brekke, Art Byrne, Jeff Chester, Jean Cunningham, Raju Deshpande, Mark Graban, Jim Huntzinger, Jeff Liker, Kevin Limbach, Brian Maskell, Kevin Meyer, John Shook, Rick Sunamoto, Daryl Tol, Daniel Wolcott, and Jerry Wright. And a very special thank you goes to Ed Gwozda who generously read the manuscript twice and provided spot-on feedback.

Another round of thank yous goes to the stellar McGraw-Hill team and their extended family, all of whom make publishing a book a far more enjoyable process than we hear from many other authors: Knox Huston, Courtney Fischer, Jane Palmieri, Maureen Harper, Mary Glenn, Scott Rattray, and to Alison Shurtz and Kristen Eberhard whose eye for detail blew us away!

Finally, a deep thank you to publishing maestro John Willig for his unwavering support and his exceptional ability to walk the talk. "Ever onward, Mr. Willig!"

Introduction

We view value stream thinking as a fundamental mindset for business success. Without it, organizations fail to develop customer-centric processes and fail to organize in a way that best serves the very reason they exist.

Value stream mapping is a practical and highly effective way to learn to see and resolve disconnects, redundancies, and gaps in how work gets done. It is not merely a tool. It's a team-based methodology that we believe is the foundation of a proven management practice. In our experience, organizations that don't use value stream mapping to understand and improve their operations are far less likely to experience outstanding performance. We believe it's been the missing link in business management and, used effectively, has the power to address many business woes. We realize that's a bold statement and a tall order to place on a single methodology. But we encourage you to suspend your disbelief until you reach the last page of this book and have experimented using value stream mapping as it was originally intended.

In 1999, the seminal work *Learning to See* was published and transformed the way many people viewed how work flows—or, more commonly, doesn't flow—through an enterprise. Authors Mike Rother and John Shook altered the course of operations design—

perhaps to an extent that even they had not anticipated. Value stream mapping presented a holistic and visual way to deeply understand how work gets done and to design an improved future state. Rother and Shook also introduced us to a more powerful process measurement framework than previous improvement methodologies had. As a result, countless organizations have changed how they deliver value to their customers, measure their performance, and design work to maximize their performance—in manufacturing.

In 2004, Beau Keyte and Drew Locher broke ground with the first book that addressed how to use value stream mapping to improve the administrative areas within manufacturing. *The Complete Lean Enterprise* not only addressed some of the nuances that need to be taken into account when analyzing, designing, and managing information-intensive settings, but it also introduced the most powerful metric we've seen for analyzing processes in office, service, and knowledge work environments: percent complete and accurate (%C&A). However, as groundbreaking as the book was in applying value stream mapping in office environments, it focused exclusively on office environments within the manufacturing sector.

The improvement community has come a long way since 2004. Owing to the continued study of and a growing body of work around what makes Toyota tick, our collective understanding about Lean management practices has deepened. Organizations in every sector are now adopting Lean principles and practices, and applying Lean tools to support those practices. We wrote this book primarily for organizations in information-intensive office, service, and knowledge work environments—communications, construction, education, energy, entertainment, financial services, food service, government, healthcare, hospitality, intelligence, law, law enforcement, military, nonprofits, publishing, real estate, research and development, retail, social services, technology, transportation, and travel and tourism sectors—and for manufacturers who wish to transform the way their office areas operate to better support the delivery of value to customers. We set out to address three significant disconnects we frequently see in organizations:

1. Many organizations remain unfamiliar with value stream mapping as a methodology, a foundation for Lean business management, and a means to build outstanding organizations. As a result, they are slower to achieve measurable improvement and to adopt customer-centric thinking.

2. Many of those organizations that have adopted value stream mapping are underutilizing the methodology because they don't fully understand the why, what, and how of the approach—especially in office, service, and knowledge work environments. Failure to involve leadership, employ cross-functional teams, and include relevant metrics, for example, often results in subpar future state designs that collect dust.

3. Many organizations are misusing value stream mapping and, as a result, not reaping the full set of benefits the approach offers. For example, using value stream mapping to map at a process level misses the entire point of value stream mapping: viewing work systems from macro-level perspectives in order to create organization-wide alignment.

It is our hope that you'll use this book to begin using value stream mapping as a means to manage your business or, for organizations with value stream mapping experience, as a resource to reflect and see how you can improve the effectiveness of your value stream mapping efforts. There are too many business problems to be solved and too many opportunities to be leveraged to operate without a highly effective means for accomplishing the important work to be done.

Some notes about this book:

1. While we wrote this book to specifically address value stream mapping in office, service, and knowledge work environments, much of the content also applies to production value streams within manufacturing. Since we've included detailed content about who should map, how mapping should be planned and conducted, and what steps need to be taken after mapping, those in manufacturing will also benefit from these considerations.

2. This book focuses on the benefits of value stream mapping, how to plan for and conduct value stream mapping activities, and how to manage value streams to sustain the gains and drive ongoing improvement. It's beyond the scope of this book to address ways for solving specific value stream problems and leveraging opportunities that may exist. While we refer to potential tools and countermeasures, they are not explained in detail. There are volumes of books written about nearly every type of Lean tool. Value stream mapping facilitators need to possess proficiency in using the full spectrum of potential countermeasures.

3. It's a challenge to write a book that every reader sees as meeting his or her very specific needs. All too often, people have difficulty applying concepts to their own environment and become overly concerned with the specifics of examples given rather than focusing on the concept itself. When we began writing this book, we planned on including value stream maps from various industries and settings in the body of the book to illustrate the how-to elements of mapping. Midway through the writing process we decided to, instead, teach the step-by-step process for creating

maps by using a generic map that could apply to any
environment. We made this decision to assure the highest
degree of learning and to minimize the distraction that
could result if a reader has difficulty seeing the conceptual
similarities, for example, between patient flow and software
development, or between litigation and designing a
commercial structure. We use the generic map throughout
the book to illustrate the progressive nature of building a
value stream map.

Recognizing the benefits of integrating actual (sanitized)
maps, we've included five sets of industry-specific value
stream maps in Appendices B–F to enable the reader to
see not only how work and information are depicted on a
map, but also the varying degrees of complexity that actual
value stream maps often have. Each Appendix includes a
current state and future state value stream map, and a table
that shows the summary metrics for the current state and
projected metrics for the future state design.

These examples represent three types of maps (full value
streams, support value streams, and value stream segments)
and illustrate the similarities and differences in maps from
different environments. Between the two of us, we've facilitated team-based value stream mapping activities (or have
advised those creating value stream maps) in nearly every
industry and environment. We believe these five examples
provide a solid foundation for you to envision how completed value stream maps in your environment could look.

While we've included an explanation for each map,
we've limited the details to those that are most relevant
for understanding "the big picture." Our intention is to
highlight the specific learning points that we feel are most
relevant. Each of the mapping activities we facilitate offers

enough fodder for detailed case studies, but that is not the intent of the Appendices.

4. For clarity, expediency, and publishing ease, we've relied on iGrafx Flowcharter to create electronic versions of the value stream maps we've included in this book. *Please don't assume that value stream maps must be put into some sort of electronic form.* On the contrary, we first create maps using paper and Post-its on a wall and recommend that you do as well. That said, digitizing a manually produced value stream map provides an easier way to share, store, and revise the maps. If your value stream map is fairly simple, taking a picture of it may be sufficient for creating an electronic means to share and store your maps. But if the map is more complex than what a photo can adequately capture or you would like the means to auto-calculate the summary metrics that are key for measuring improvement, software becomes your friend. There are several other software options available for documenting value stream maps electronically. We prefer iGrafx.

This book offers a series of guidelines (versus hard-and-fast rules) that we've found to deepen results and accelerate improvement. Some of these guidelines relate to actual mapping conventions, whereas others relate to leadership engagement, the sequence of events, mapping execution, and deploying the future state design. As with any methodology, you may need to adapt our perspective to suit your environment. That said, make sure that your reasons for adaptation are sound and that you aren't rejecting new mindsets and behaviors that would allow you to reap the greatest benefits that value stream mapping offers.

One final note—and it's a caution: Please keep in mind that, while tools are necessary for performance improvement, they are not sufficient. Rather than viewing value stream mapping as just a tool to reduce operational waste, the broader use of value stream mapping as a methodology to transform leadership thinking, define strategy and priorities, and assure that customers are receiving high levels of value (versus focusing merely on reducing operational waste) is where value stream mapping earns its brightest stripes.

Now let's dig in. There's much to learn.

1

Value Stream Management

In most organizations, no one person can describe the complete series of events required to transform a customer request into a good or service—at least not with any level of detail around organizational performance. This gap in understanding is the kind of problem that leads to making improvements in one functional area only to create new problems in another area. It's the kind of problem that results in adding processes that increase operational cost but doesn't truly solve problems with root causes that reside upstream. It's the kind of problem that propels well-meaning companies to implement expensive technology "solutions" that do little to address the true problem or improve the customer experience.

The lack of understanding about how work flows—or, more commonly, doesn't flow—across a work system that's sole purpose is to deliver value to a customer is a fundamental problem that results in poor performance, poor business decisions, and poor work environments. Conflicting priorities, interdepartmental tension, and—in the worst cases—infighting within leadership teams are common outcomes when a company attempts to operate without a clear understanding about how an organization's various parts fit together and how value is delivered to its customers. And significant time and money is wasted when organizations attempt to make improvement without a clearly defined, externally focused improvement strategy that places the customer in the center. Enter the concepts of value streams and value stream mapping.

WHAT IS A VALUE STREAM?

The term *value stream* was coined by James Womack, Daniel Jones, and Daniel Roos in the book that launched the Lean movement, *The Machine that Changed the World* (1990), and further popularized by James Womack and Daniel Jones in *Lean Thinking* (1996). A value stream is the sequence of activities an organization undertakes to deliver on a customer request. More broadly, a value stream is the sequence of activities required to design, produce, and deliver a good or service to a customer, and it includes the dual flows of information and material. Most value streams are highly cross-functional: the transformation of a customer request to a good or service flows through many functional departments or work teams within the organization.

An extended value stream includes those activities that precede a customer order (e.g., responding to a request for a quote, determining market needs, developing new products, etc.) or occur following the delivery of a good or service to a customer (e.g., billing and processing payments or submitting required compliance reports).

While many of a value stream's activities occur sequentially, others may be performed concurrently (in parallel) to other work. The activities in a value stream are not merely those that an organization performs itself: work done by outside parties and even the customers themselves are part of a value stream.

Value streams come in many forms. The primary type of value stream is one in which a good or service is requested by and delivered to an external customer. Other value streams support the delivery of value; we often refer to these as *value-enabling* or *support value streams*. Examples of support value streams include recruiting, hiring, and onboarding; IT support; the annual budgeting process; and the sales cycle. Complex creative work can be viewed as having its own value stream—from initial concept to an executable design or to product launch. Product design can be viewed as a *value stream segment* if the design is required to fulfill a specific customer order.

Many value streams can go on and on in both directions. For example, a value stream could include all of the activities from the time a customer selects an architect until drawings are delivered to a general contractor. Or until construction planning is complete. Or until the final inspection after a structure has been built. Or until revenue has been collected for the construction work. The product life cycle is also a value stream consisting of specification, design, supply chain, manufacture, commissioning, operation, and ultimately decommissioning and disposal. A full value stream for patient care might include appointment scheduling, registration, diagnosis, treatment, aftercare, and possibly even receipt of payment. As you'll learn in Chapter 2, one of the first steps you'll take in preparing to analyze a value stream is defining the scope—the "fence posts" or beginning and ending points for review. This will depend largely on the problems you need to address or the performance improvements you would like to realize.

So how many value streams does an organization have? It varies. Small organizations may have only one customer-facing value stream and many internal support value streams. Large organizations could have 5, 10, or even dozens of customer-facing value streams and hundreds of support value streams. Wherever there is a request and a deliverable, there is a value stream.

One way to determine how many value streams your organization has is by looking at the types of internal and external customer requests your organization receives and the number of variants of high-level process flows that each of those requests pass through.* Requests that pass through similar process flow sequences form a single "product family." To reap the greatest gains from viewing work and organizing the business according to value streams, you will eventually want to analyze and improve each product family's value stream. The best methodology we've found to date for this effort is *value stream mapping*, a tool that helps you visualize complex work systems so you can address the disconnects, redundancies, and gaps in how work gets done. Used properly, value stream mapping is far more than a design tool: it's the most powerful organization transformation tool we've seen to date. Once people learn how to think in value stream terms, it's difficult for them to look at work in any other way.

What Is Value Stream Mapping?

The roots of value stream mapping can be traced to a visual mapping technique used at the Toyota Motor Corporation known as "material and information flows." As the West grew intrigued with Toyota's consistent track record and began studying how Toyota's approach differed from its own, we learned that Toyota's focus on

---

*It bears repeating: a value stream is a sequence of processes and activities an organization undertakes to fulfill a customer request. Functional departments (e.g., marketing, finance, community relations, IT) and desired outcomes (e.g., safety, high quality, regulatory compliance, employee engagement, and improved communication) are *not* value streams. Value streams typically cut across functional departments and produce a specific deliverable based on a customer request or regularly scheduled need (e.g., scheduled maintenance or an annual financial audit).

understanding the material and information flow across the organization was a significant contributor to its ability to perform at
consistently high levels. As a result, mapping these types of flows
became one of the hallmark approaches used in the Lean movement
to transform operations. But value stream mapping is neither clearly
understood nor effectively utilized in all circles. To understand why,
a little history is in order.

Lean is a term that means different things to different people,
which is one reason why companies, government agencies, and not-
for-profit organizations have experienced such wide-ranging results
from exploring and adopting Lean practices. When you look at the
history of how Lean was introduced in the West and the degree to
which our collective understanding of this management approach
has evolved, you can see why there's confusion about what Lean is
and what it is not.

The term *Lean* was coined by John Krafcik in a 1988 article based
on his master's thesis at MIT Sloan School of Management[1] and
then popularized in *The Machine that Changed the World* and *Lean
Thinking. Lean Thinking* summarized Womack and Jones's findings
from studying how Toyota operates, an approach that was spear-
headed by Taiichi Ohno, codified by Shigeo Shingo, and strongly
influenced by the work of W. Edwards Deming, Joseph Juran, Henry
Ford, and U.S. grocery stores. *Lean Thinking* framed Toyota's philosophical and operational bias around five key principles—value, the
value stream, flow, pull, and perfection—and launched an era where
thousands of companies attempted to mimic how Toyota operated.
The Toyota Production System (TPS)—or Lean, as TPS and its newer
iteration, Toyota Business Practices (TBP) are commonly referred
to—became the darling of an army of consultants, authors, and
improvement professionals.

While *Lean Thinking* provided a powerful foundation in understanding the basic concepts related to the actual delivery of value,

several of the most pressing topics in Lean circles today—leadership practices, culture, problem solving, and coaching—weren't explicitly addressed. This isn't a criticism of Womack and Jones's transformative work; they were clearly at the leading edge of this revolution in management thinking. But, two decades later, we can now look back and see how little Lean academics, consultants, and practitioners collectively understood at that time about the full range of philosophical underpinnings and management practices that have contributed to Toyota's ongoing success. As more and more people and organizations studied and adapted Toyota's methods, new discoveries surfaced.

Eight years later, Jeffrey Liker published *The Toyota Way* (2004), which was the first comprehensive look into how Toyota operates in terms of its philosophy, processes, people, and problem solving approach. While this pivotal work included an explanation of the mechanistic aspects of operations design, Liker's background in sociology propelled him to dig more deeply into the cultural and leadership elements at play. Liker organized his findings into 14 management principles that captured the essence of Toyota's organizational and business practices.

However, even with this expanded view of the foundational elements that produce consistently high levels of performance, many had difficulty seeing the core beliefs and behaviors that allowed Toyota to perform to these levels, thrive when times were good, and to bounce back quickly when faced with difficulties. Perhaps our Western minds couldn't grasp a management approach that most of us had never experienced firsthand. Or perhaps we naturally gravitate to mechanistic solutions because they are concrete. After all, dealing with people is complicated and messy. Part of the reason may lie with those consultants who—even after Lean literature was replete with information about the vital role leadership, problem solving, and daily improvement played in transformation—continued to focus on tools-based "implementation" versus people-based transformation. Whatever the reason, for many, their love affair with tools continued.

Value stream mapping was embraced as one such tool. Authors Mike Rother and John Shook studied Toyota's "material and information flow mapping" and recast the method as "value stream mapping" in the landmark book *Learning to See* (1999). The result of Rother's studies and Shook's 10 years of experience in a leadership role at Toyota, *Learning to See* provided us with the first tangible method for "seeing" the value streams that Womack et. al defined. After using value stream mapping for over 10 years to transform operations in nearly every industry, we believe it's the most powerful, yet under-utilized improvement "tool" we've seen to date. But the power behind value stream mapping lies in a little understood reality: it's far more than just a tool.

Value stream maps offer a holistic view of how work flows through entire systems, and they differ from process maps in several significant ways. First, value stream maps provide an effective means to establish a strategic direction for making improvement. The inclination to jump into the weeds and design micro-level improvements before the entire work system—the macro picture—is fully understood, is a key contributor to suboptimization.* As shown in Figure 1.1, work has various degrees of granularity. Value stream mapping, the macro perspective, provides the means for leadership to define strategic improvements to the work flow, whereas process-level mapping† enables the people who do the work to design tactical

---

*Suboptimization occurs when you make an improvement to one component of a system while ignoring the effects of that change on the other components. A seemingly important improvement could cause the overall work system to perform more poorly. For example, if one department successfully reduces its turnaround time, but the faster output merely causes a larger queue and/or more work for the downstream department, the improvement may have a negative impact on the performance of the overall system.

† See our earlier work, *Metrics-Based Process Mapping* (Productivity Press, 2013) for our preferred process mapping technique. The book includes a CD with an Excel-based tool for documenting processes and calculating results.

improvements. As you'll learn about in the next chapter, this difference signals the need for a higher-level value stream mapping team than what many organizations often think they need.

FIGURE 1.1 Granularity of work

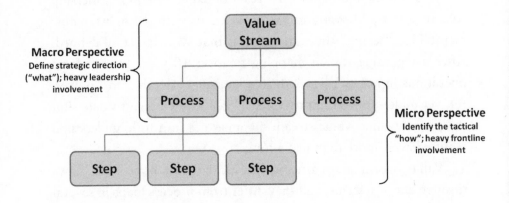

Second, value stream maps provide a highly visual, full-cycle view—a storyboard—of how work progresses from a request of some sort to fulfilling that request. This cycle can be described as request to receipt, order to delivery, ring to ring (phone call to cash register), cradle to grave, or quote to cash. A cyclical view places the customer (who is typically both the requester and recipient) in a central position, which provides a powerful means to view an entire work system as it relates to delivering customer value. As shown in Figure 1.2, visually depicting the cycle of work typically includes three components: information flow, work flow, and a summary timeline. Chapter 3 will describe each component in detail.

Third, the process of value stream mapping deepens organizational understanding about the work systems that deliver value and support the delivery of value to customers, which aids in better decision making and work design. By distilling complex systems

FIGURE 1.2 Basic current state value stream map

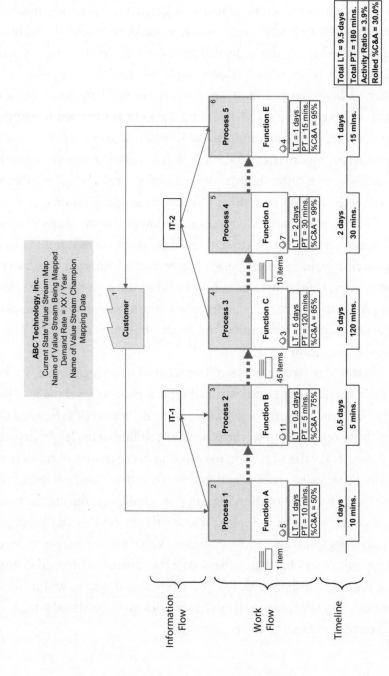

into simpler and higher-level components that can be understood by everyone from senior leaders to the front lines, organizations create common ground from which to make decisions. In addition, the mental shaping that's needed to succinctly define complex work systems is a boon when redesigning work to deliver greater value, faster, at lower cost, and in safer and more fulfilling work environments. There's a logistics advantage as well: value stream mapping enables a team to fully understand how work flows through a complex system in a matter of days, whereas detailed process mapping (which serves a different purpose) can take weeks or months and is too detailed to help in making effective strategic decisions.

Fourth, the quantitative nature of value stream maps provides the foundation for data-driven, strategic decision making. Measuring overall value stream performance and identifying the barriers and process breakdowns as the work flows through the value stream is a powerful way to drive continuous improvement so that an organization is able to better meet the needs of both its customers and its internal operation.

Last, value stream maps reflect work flow as a customer experiences it versus the internal focus of typical process-level maps. Many organizations are structured as a series of function-based silos that bear little relationship to the customer fulfillment cycle. As depicted in Figure 1.3, value stream maps force an organization to think holistically in terms of cross-functional work systems and product families. While this type of thinking can pose challenges during the future state design phase of mapping, it's exactly the type of challenge progressive organizations must embrace. Value stream mapping forces an organization's hand to either make the difficult structural changes that are more in line with the cross-functional reality within which they exist, or continue to deny reality, stick with outdated structures, and continue to perform accordingly.

FIGURE 1.3 Vertical organization structure versus horizontal reality

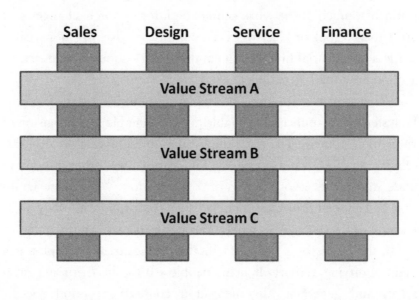

THE BENEFITS OF VALUE STREAM MAPPING

It bears repeating: the benefits of well-executed value stream mapping go far beyond how it's commonly but narrowly viewed: as a work flow design tool. While organizations rightfully turn to value stream mapping to serve a specific end (an improved value stream), they often miss the ample transformational opportunities that have longer-lasting and deeper benefits than the mapping results themselves. Transformation requires fundamental changes in an organization's DNA; done well, value stream mapping can be instrumental in facilitating the necessary shifts in mindsets and behaviors.

Visual Unification Tool

While value stream maps are powerful tools in improving manufacturing production work flows, they are arguably even more powerful when used to visualize work that's not particularly visual to begin with. In most office, service, creative, and knowledge work environments, much of the work centers on information exchanges that are either verbal or electronic. The ability to visualize non-visible work is an essential first step in gaining clarity about and consensus around how work gets done.

Value stream mapping is particularly useful for visualizing how IT systems and applications enable (or don't enable) the provision of value to customers. The mapping process often reveals disconnects, redundancies, and unnecessary complication that otherwise aren't understood by everyone across the organization. We've seen significant and sudden project and budget shifts occur in technology areas because of the discoveries gained through value stream mapping.

In the hands of a skilled facilitator, value stream mapping is a highly unifying activity. It helps people see the need for improvement, and generates alignment and consensus around specific improvements being considered. The organization-wide clarity that results from gaining a cross-functional, fact-based understanding of the current state begins the process of identifying and accepting the need for change. Future state value stream maps (shown in Figure 1.4 and described in detail in Chapter 4) and the resulting transformation plans (described in Chapter 5) also serve as effective leadership alignment tools that improve organizational focus and reduce the risk of two departments moving in conflicting directions. The visual nature of value stream maps enables consensus-building conversations across the organization, from the front lines to senior leaders.

Connection to the Customer

Value stream maps provide a clear line of sight to the external customer from every function and work area involved in the value stream. This degree of clarity helps an organization make the transition from internally focused thinking to customer-focused thinking, which is the foundation for providing greater and greater value.

FIGURE 1.4 Basic future state value stream map

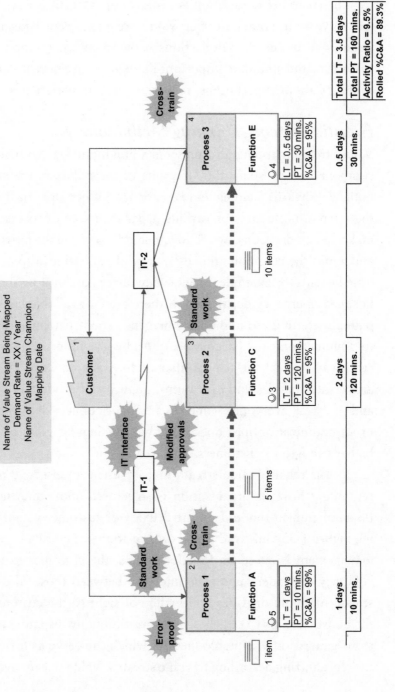

ABC Technology, Inc.
Future State Value Stream Map
Name of Value Stream Being Mapped
Demand Rate = XX / Year
Name of Value Stream Champion
Mapping Date

Customer

Error proof

Standard work

Cross-train

IT interface

Modified approvals

Standard work

Cross-train

IT-1

IT-2

1 item

5 items

10 items

Process 1
Function A
○5
LT = 1 days
PT = 10 mins.
%C&A = 99%

Process 2
Function C
○3
LT = 2 days
PT = 120 mins.
%C&A = 95%

Process 3
Function E
○4
LT = 0.5 days
PT = 30 mins.
%C&A = 95%

1 days / 10 mins.
2 days / 120 mins.
0.5 days / 30 mins.

Total LT = 3.5 days
Total PT = 160 mins.
Activity Ratio = 9.5%
Rolled %C&A = 89.3%

13

The customer connection is no less important in value streams that serve an internal customer. Value stream maps provide a highly visual way to see the connections between internal suppliers and customers and stimulate important dialogue between customers and suppliers about expectations, requirements, and preferences.

Holistic Systems-Thinking Methodology

Value stream mapping also presents a pragmatic way to realize key components of systems thinking, one of the pillars in the work of both W. Edwards Deming and Peter Senge.[2] When organizations see the interconnectedness of various departments and processes, they make better decisions, work together in more collaborative ways, and avoid the common and costly trap of suboptimization. There's little benefit, for example, in achieving faster patient flow through a hospital emergency department if there are no available beds in the patient care units to admit an emergency room patient into owing to a cumbersome discharge process. And we've found no more powerful way to heal the tension that often exists between functional areas, such as sales and operations, quality and production, and IT and . . . well, everyone! Value stream maps connect disparate parts of an organization into one whole with a singular goal: providing higher value to its customers.

In this regard, value stream maps present an effective tool for rethinking how an organization is structured and achieving functional alignment that aids in the delivery of customer value. Recalling Figure 1.3, while traditional organization structure and business management is based on functional silos, the customer experience is largely dependent upon the interplay between those silos. Value stream mapping provides a clear line of sight to the customer and the holistic means to clearly see how traditionally disparate parts of the organization are interconnected, which can serve as the catalyst for reorganizing according to value streams. Value stream maps also provide unbiased, fact-based insight into how processes should be managed to achieve and sustain high levels of performance.

Simplification Tool

Business has grown increasingly complex, making value stream maps all the more relevant for managing business. Nearly every industry and organization is coping with increasingly high degrees of variation in customer types, needs, and expectations; inputs to the system; the process for producing outputs from the system; the features and functionality of the outputs themselves; the parties involved between the organization and the end user of a good or service; the location of those parties; and so on. Product customization is also on the rise. Value stream maps are powerful tools for visualizing and simplifying how work gets done at a macro level in order to make better and faster strategic improvement decisions.

The exercise of distilling complex work systems to their most essential and macro-level components builds critical thinking skills and creates a more manageable means for designing improvements to an entire system. Similarly, the process of defining "product families" (described in Chapter 2) helps people see commonality versus difference, a unifying discovery that can accelerate problem resolution and reduce resistance to change. For many organizations, creating these visual storyboards is the first time any one person has understood the entire work flow. Value stream mapping, done well, develops that degree of insight in *many* people. As Deming is commonly reported to have said, "If you can't describe what you are doing as a process, you don't know what you're doing." We'll take that quote a step further: if you can't describe what you're doing as a value stream, you don't know what you're doing. Value stream maps provide this clarity.

Value stream maps also counter the psychological tendency to feel that your world is more complex than any other and that it's almost unmanageable. Very few things are unmanageable once they are distilled to their basic components. When you can gain alignment from people about how the basic components should operate at a macro level, you've taken a giant leap forward in gaining alignment about the specifics and creating ease in designing the specifics to meet a defined "macro" state.

Practical Means to Drive Continuous Improvement

Value stream mapping becomes an important step in using the Plan-Do-Study-Adjust (PDSA) cycle* to solve performance issues, capitalize on market opportunities, plan new product lines, and improve existing ones. The iterative and repetitive nature of improvement shown in Figure 1.5 is best served by tying improvement to a larger strategy. The future state value stream map provides the strategic framework (a blueprint) within which to make tactical improvement.

FIGURE 1.5 Cycles of continuous improvement

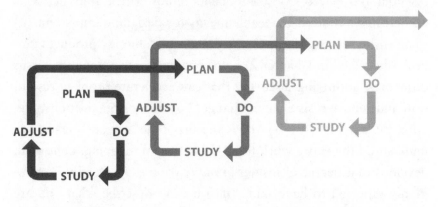

---

*The PDSA (plan-do-study-adjust) cycle is one of several scientific methods for problem solving, making improvements, and designing work of all types. We use PDSA throughout this book, but you may substitute PDCA (plan-do-check-act), DMAIC (define-measure-analyze-improve-control), Ford's 8D methodology, or any other cyclical scientific improvement method in its place. For more details about the PDSA cycle, see Karen's book *The Outstanding Organization* (McGraw-Hill, 2012) or any number of improvement-related books.

For this reason, value stream maps are highly iterative tools that need to be frequently consulted and updated as the value stream changes. We recommend physically posting the maps in strategic locations and holding regular stand-up meetings to discuss value stream performance and drive ongoing improvement. Value stream maps should not merely reside on shared drives. They are working blueprints for how your organization functions and should drive discussions and decision making at all levels.

Effective Means to Orient New Hires

Value stream maps also serve as a simple visual means to orient new hires during the onboarding process. Helping people understand where they fit in an organization fills a fundamental need all human beings have for connection and begins instilling holistic thinking from an employee's first day of work. Similar to a map in an airport or shopping mall that says, "You are here," value stream maps show employees how they fit into the larger picture and provide clarity about how the company operates. Organizations who seek to provide greater customer value need to make sure that every single employee understands his or her connection to the customer. Orienting new hires to value stream thinking the moment they arrive also serves the important goal of building a continuous improvement culture.

If you use the methods in this book to plan and execute value stream mapping, you will experience not only measurable improvement in how work gets done, but also significant cultural shifts. It's the *process* of value stream mapping rather than the maps themselves that carries the greatest power by instilling transformational mindsets and behaviors into the DNA of an organization. Effectively done, value stream mapping changes how people think and act, how they interact with one another, and how they view work. Problem solving has richer conclusions, and the solutions are longer lasting. Customers are happier. The work environment is less stressful, more fulfilling, and safer. And, assuming that customers place high value on the goods or services they're receiving, improvements that begin with a value stream perspective are more likely to be sustained and lead to both top-line and bottom-line growth. In the case of government agencies and nonprofit organizations, proper value stream design and management can reduce costs, improve organizational effectiveness, reduce the risk of privatization, free up cash to reinvest in the agency, and improve employee morale and constituent satisfaction.

COMMON FAILINGS WITH VALUE STREAM MAPPING

To fully leverage the power of value stream mapping, we recommend you avoid these common failings:

Using the Mapping Process Solely as a Work Design Exercise

One of the failings we often see is value stream maps being used mechanistically as a tool solely to improve value stream performance. While that's an important reason to map, going through the effort of creating value stream maps without experiencing its accompanying organizational learning, culture shifts, and leadership development benefits is like buying a Ferrari and using it only for city driving where the speed limit is 35 miles per hour.

Using the Map to Make Tactical Improvements

Too many organizations miss the benefits of value stream mapping by trying to use them to define tactical-level improvements, the purview of process maps. One visual cue that this problem exists is when we see so-called value stream maps that extend the entire length of a wall, containing 30, 50, or even more process steps. Another visual cue is when the maps are formatted in swim lanes and/or are missing information flow. While it's true that many value stream maps—or portions of value stream maps—may need to be "drilled down" before actual improvement can be designed, tested, and implemented, that's the domain for process-level maps: defining the micro details about *how* specifically the macro-level change should be designed, tested, and implemented. The two types of maps serve two very different purposes.

People often ask us how to determine when they should use value stream mapping and when they should turn to process-level mapping. While it's situational, we nearly always begin with value stream mapping to align leadership and set priorities. We often turn to process mapping for those sections of the value stream that require deeper exploration and for creating standard work, an improvement requirement that requires more specificity than a value stream map provides.

*Creating Value Stream Maps During a Kaizen Event**

Related to the first two common failings is using a kaizen event as a venue for creating value stream maps. By nature, the two activities have different purposes and intended outcomes, require different people, and follow a different process. We regularly use process mapping in kaizen events, whereas value stream mapping typically precedes kaizen events. Let us be clear: kaizen events are a specific format for designing, testing, and implementing actual improvement, whereas a value stream mapping activity's purpose is to create a plan and alignment for improvement. Value stream mapping activities are strategic; kaizen events are tactical. Kaizen events should be heavily biased with the people who *do* the work being improved, and value stream mapping activities should be heavily biased with the people who *oversee* the work being improved.

*Kaizen events are two- to five-day focused improvement activities during which a sequestered, cross-functional team designs and fully implements improvements to a defined process or work area. See *The Kaizen Event Planner* (Martin and Osterling, Productivity Press, 2007) for more information and to obtain a set of Excel-based planning and execution tools.

Creating Maps but Taking No Action

All too often we see organizations with beautifully designed current state value stream maps but no future state value stream maps. Or beautifully designed future state maps, but no action plan for realizing the future state. Or a detailed plan, but no significant action being taken to achieve the future state. Again, the purpose of value stream mapping is to improve the value stream. Many organizations need to move beyond where they often have the greatest comfort—analysis and design—and become far better at execution.

We do, however, have one rare exception to this rule. There are times when it can be beneficial to create a current state value stream map solely to build urgency for improvement or achieving clarity and "thought alignment" across a leadership team. For example, we've worked with organizations where the leadership team was so far apart in terms of priorities or even the need for improvement that we turned to current state value stream mapping as a learning and alignment tool. By gaining a fundamental understanding of the interconnectedness—or the lack thereof—that exists across the organization, leaders make better decisions, are more tolerant of each other's pain points, and become more collaborative in solving organizational problems. And seeing the undeniable need for improvement makes it more difficult for resistant leaders to ignore the need for change.

Some people may balk at using value stream maps this way, and we'd be lying if we didn't say that it concerns us to see mapping stop at the current state. After all, once an organization has clarity about how work flows (or, more commonly, doesn't flow), the natural next step is to use this knowledge to make improvements. So if you're tempted to create current state value stream maps to deepen understanding and achieve an alignment objective, lobby hard to take it to the next step: designing an improved value stream and then making it happen. As Goethe asserted, "Knowing is not enough; we must apply. Willing is not enough; we must do."[3]

Mapping with an Inappropriate Team—or No Team at All

Related to the danger of using value stream maps at a process level, many organizations miss the richness that comes from having the appropriate parties on the mapping team. Since value stream mapping is a strategic improvement activity and the future state map often requires significant organizational change, the team must include those individuals who can authorize that level of change. As you'll learn more about in Chapter 2, if no one on the team has the authority to make the changes, the future state map and transformation plan must go through a "sales" process, which can delay the initiation of improvements by weeks or months, or even stall them permanently. In addition to the risk of delayed action, the quality of decisions often suffers when leaders who can authorize change aren't present to witness the reality of the current state, feel the pain firsthand, and participate in the discussions that contribute to a team's decision that X or Y needs to occur. In our experience, postmapping sales processes often devolve into a game of gossip, with the leader who can authorize change reversing the team's decisions because he or she doesn't fully grasp the reasons behind those decisions.

While it's a significant time commitment for leaders to serve as members of a value stream mapping team, it's by far the most effective and expedient way for an organization to initiate the transformation to improved performance. And we've found it's a highly effective means to shape leadership mindsets and behaviors in a way that accelerates organizational transformation. We'll return to leadership's role in Chapter 2.

Even worse is delegating value stream map creation to an individual. Value stream mapping is a team sport. A baseball team's not going to win many games if the pitcher's the only one practicing. *Learning to See*, the apt title for the first book about value stream mapping, says it all. It does little good for an organization to have one person learning to see, especially if that person is a full-time improvement professional. And having one person decide how work should be done at a strategic level is a recipe for disaster.

Creating Maps with No Metrics*

As we mentioned earlier in the chapter, a typical value stream map has three key components: information flow, work flow, and a time-line. Using time to drive improvement has proven one of the greatest contributions the Lean movement has brought to the operations design table. The timeline is, by extension, where value stream mapping shines its brightest light. Using a "ticking clock" to measure throughput and the time it takes for people to actually perform work tasks reveals more about work flow than any analytical tool to date. And, as we mentioned in the Introduction and you'll learn about more in Chapter 3, the quality metric, percent complete and accurate (%C&A), provides powerful insight into errors being made that introduce organizational chaos, add cost, cause frustration, delay delivery, and, in some environments, cause injury or death.

Unfortunately, we frequently see "value stream maps" with no metrics on them at all. This again calls to mind the Ferrari analogy: underutilization of a high-powered machine. How do you measure whether you've made improvements without a baseline from which to measure? How do you know what to focus on if you don't know how the value stream truly performs? While a picture's worth a thousand words, value stream maps without metrics have limited use. And one could argue that value stream maps without metrics aren't value stream maps at all.

That said, as we mentioned earlier, we do occasionally use current state value stream mapping to accomplish very specific objec-

---

*Metrics are performance measures that are used to set goals, reflect current conditions, show trends, provide warnings, drive corrective action, and design and measure improvement. They're a means for tracking performance against goals.

tives, such as heightening awareness about how disparate parts of an organization connect to create the whole. We've also led mapping efforts that are designed solely to help inwardly thinking leaders see the value of looking at work from a customer's perspective. But if your intent is improvement, a map without metrics leaves you with no foundation from which to measure your success, nor a defined target to guide a team's design efforts.

WHERE SHOULD YOU BEGIN?

One of the most frequently asked questions we get from people in organizations that see the value of Lean management practices and are eager to begin reaping the benefits is, "Where should we begin?" A closely related question is, "When should we create value stream maps?" The answer to these questions depends on many factors. Ideally, an organization seeking transformation already has a clearly defined purpose, consensus around its strategic direction, clearly defined business goals, and alignment around a limited number of improvement priorities that are needed to meet or exceed its business goals for that fiscal year. If it doesn't, adopting the practice of strategy deployment* is a wise foundational step before the organization gets too far down the value stream mapping path. The practice of strategy deployment enables an organization to create an action plan that focuses on a limited number of problems to be solved and/or opportunities to be leveraged. Once the problems and opportunities are clearly defined, the value streams that must be improved become rather obvious.

---

*Strategy deployment is a method for defining and gaining consensus around the priorities needed to realize an organization's business goals. Developed in the 1950s, it's also referred to as policy deployment and *hoshin kanri*. For more information, see Pascal Dennis's *Getting the Right Things Done* (The Lean Enterprise Institute, 2006) and Thomas Jackson's *Hoshin Kanri for the Lean Enterprise* (Productivity Press, 2006). See Karen's *The Outstanding Organization* (McGraw-Hill, 2012) for a modified version of strategy deployment.

If your organization doesn't have a disciplined approach to setting annual goals and defining a limited number of priorities (and remaining focused on both), and you aren't in the position to influence the development of such behavior, you may want to experiment with value stream mapping by selecting a value stream that is suffering from one or more performance problems, such as slow delivery, customer complaints, regulatory noncompliance, cost overruns, waning productivity, safety violations, low morale, and so on. We also recommend taking a look at the full value stream any time an organization experiences eroding margins; faces new competition or market share loss; or, on the positive side, wishes to improve operations to increase a company's market value.

Another situation that may call for value stream mapping arises when, during the course of problem solving using A3 management,* a team needs to gain high-level clarity about how work flows across many functions or work teams. In this case, value stream mapping becomes an option for gaining the necessary understanding to surface problems and identify the root causes for those problems.†

We also recommend value stream mapping as a fundamental tool for improving overall responsiveness to customers, designing and rolling out new product lines (including the development process on the front end and the service process on the back end), forming partnerships and joint ventures, integrating acquired operations, and as a required predecessor activity before any sort of organization

---

*A3 is an effective and systematic means for developing people and building strong organization-wide problem-solving capacities. For more information, see *Managing to Learn* (Shook, The Lean Enterprise Institute, 2008) and *Understanding A3 Thinking* (Sobek and Smalley, Productivity Press, 2008).

†The opposite is also true: the process of value stream improvement could spawn the need for A3 problem solving, a situation you'll understand more fully by building familiarity and proficiency with A3 management. Organizations that have developed a strong A3 culture may wish to use the A3 approach to define and track their value stream transformation activities.

redesign is contemplated. In the latter case, value stream mapping can protect you from making decisions using outdated paradigms, such as the common generalizations that "functional departments are more efficient," "economies of scale will drive down costs," and "centralization is better." These cookie-cutter beliefs may or may not be the case; value stream mapping is an effective tool for deeply exploring the pros and cons of centralization and decentralization, and for clarifying functional roles and responsibilities. Companies that reorganize without understanding their value streams may experience short-term improvement, but longer-term gains are far more likely by using value stream thinking to shape the reorganization. After all, if you don't truly understand what needs to be done, how can you design an organization that satisfies those needs?

The bottom line about where to begin and when to map is that it often depends on organizational maturity and experience with Lean principles and improvement. Less experienced organizations may want to begin by identifying a value stream that could benefit from improvement, isn't too complex, has a motivated executive sponsor, and is highly visible. More mature organizations may want to conduct value stream mapping as part of their strategy deployment process. In either case, value stream mapping is a powerful discovery and design tool for addressing value stream–related problems or for raising the bar and improving performance to build a stronger organization, stay ahead of the competition, and continue the journey to optimal performance. We define optimal performance as delivering customer value in a way in which the organization incurs no unnecessary expense; the work flows without delays; the organization is 100 percent compliant with all local, state, and federal laws; the organization meets (and, ideally, exceeds) all customer-defined requirements; and employees are safe and treated with respect. Value stream mapping is an important strategic tool for achieving outstanding performance on all fronts.

Assuming your organization is ready to benefit from value stream mapping's ability to align the organization, identify the important work to be done, and improve the customer experience, the first step is planning the activity, the subject of Chapter 2.

NOTES

1. John Krafcik, "Triumph of the Lean Production System," *Sloan Management Review* 30 (1), Fall 1988, pp. 41–52.
2. See W. Edwards Deming's *Out of the Crisis* (MIT Press, 2000) and Peter M. Senge's *The Fifth Discipline* (Doubleday, 1990).
3. Thinkexist, John Wolfgang von Goethe, http://thinkexist.com/quotes/johann_wolfgang_von_goethe/.

2

Setting the Stage and Enabling Success

Too many organizations dive into value stream mapping before the organization is properly prepared and the activity has been properly scoped. Effective planning is a significant contributor in elevating value stream mapping from a "tool" to a management practice that produces long-lasting transformation.

Planning ranges from preparing the organization for the paradigm-challenging aspects of value stream mapping to scoping, team formation, and planning the logistics of who, what, when, and where. The planning stage represents the "P" in a macro-level PDSA (plan-do-study-adjust) cycle. As such, it warrants the time and attention to detail that makes for successful resolution of any problem, improvement, or execution of any project undergoing a proper PDSA cycle.

The first decision you need to make is how to structure your mapping activity. We recommend a three-phase approach that we find highly effective. As noted in Figure 2.1, we recommend that you begin planning for the mapping approximately at least four weeks prior to the mapping activity itself. That will allow you ample time to develop a charter (described in a later section), build leadership support, form a proper team, collect relevant data, and prepare your organization for the process of value stream transformation. This chapter addresses the "prepare" step. Chapters 3 and 4 show you the mechanics of creating current and future state value stream maps, and Chapters 5 and 6 outline how to develop and execute a value stream transformation plan.

FIGURE 2.1 Value stream mapping phases and timing

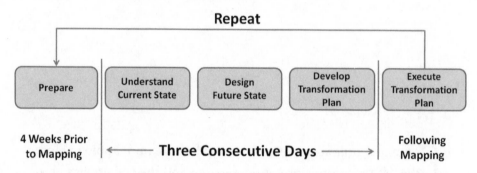

For medium to complex value streams, we have found it most helpful to create the maps and develop a transformation plan over three consecutive days, during which the team focuses on three distinct improvement phases: discovery, design, and planning. The three-day model leverages the benefits of deep focus. If you introduce gaps into the process, you break the team's momentum and introduce the need for mental rework when the team members reconvene and need to remember where they left off and why they made the decisions they did. The longer the break between sessions, the more rework the team will encounter. And it's tough enough to get a high-level mapping team together even once. Scheduling becomes more and more difficult each time you need that same team to reconvene.

The mapping activity results in three deliverables: a current state value stream map, a future state value stream map, and a value stream transformation plan. While Figure 2.1 indicates a clean break between the activities needed to produce those three deliverables, it's not uncommon for the current state mapping to extend into the first hour or two of Day 2, or for future state mapping to extend into the first hour or two of Day 3.

Executing the value stream transformation plan should begin as soon as the mapping activity ends. As we'll address later in the chapter, the execution time frame is determined while you're preparing a mapping charter. But before we address charter formation, let's step back for a moment and consider the preparation your organization may need, especially before its first value stream mapping activity.

LAYING THE GROUNDWORK

Remember that, in many cases, organizations have never studied the way they work all the way from an initial customer request to delivering on that request—and, in some cases, to payment for the good or service delivered. Or, if they have, they've operated at such a micro level that it was difficult for anyone to see how the entire work system fits together. Getting tangled up in the weeds is a common reason why process improvement efforts fail to deliver sustainable results, and why inserting value stream mapping into the improvement process helps an organization make faster and deeper progress.

From cultural considerations and organizational readiness to the mechanics of value stream mapping, many factors need to be taken into account long before you begin creating actual value stream maps. For the greatest success, it's critical that you provide an overview of value stream mapping to the mapping team and as many of your leaders as possible. We also recommend that the mapping team have at least a foundational understanding of Lean principles and some of the more common countermeasures; designing a future state without the team members possessing at least rudimentary Lean knowledge can present a bit of a challenge.

If the ripple effect of the projected improvements is somewhat contained, you can limit the overview to the team members and those leaders who oversee the areas within the value stream being transformed. If the projected improvement(s) will touch a large percentage of the workforce, it's best to include the entire leadership team. For your first few value stream mapping activities, it's also helpful to include leadership from support services, such as human resources, information technology, and finance so that they, too, can begin to see the interconnectedness within the organization and the benefits of viewing work through a value stream lens. Ultimately, every leader needs to understand the organization's key value streams and how his or her team supports the delivery of value to external customers.

The overview should include an indoctrination into what value streams are, the purpose of value stream mapping, what benefits it offers, how it's done, and what effect the activity will have on the organization. It should also explain the vital role of daily briefings (explained later in this chapter) and the roles the team members, the briefing attendees, and the facilitator will play in the briefings.

The overview can be delivered either before the charter is created, which will ease the process of creating the charter, or it can be delivered after the charter is in draft or final form. Waiting until the charter is created to deliver the overview adds real-world specificity to the overview content and the discussions it generates.

If the overview is delivered before the charter is complete, the mapping team also needs to attend a more specific session to review the charter in detail to set context and expectations, clarify scope, discuss roles and responsibilities, establish the rules of engagement, and address logistics. Ideally, this session is held prior to mapping so the team can begin mapping as soon as possible on Day 1 of the activity. If the team members and/or facilitator aren't local and a virtual overview isn't possible, the overview can be given during the first hour or two of the first day of the mapping activity, but it does cut into mapping time.

Another key success factor is exposing middle managers and the front lines to the concept of value streams. The more people begin to view work holistically (how they connect with the customer and how their work is interconnected to everyone else's), the more engaged everyone will become in understanding the customer and the business, the better decisions will be, and the less you'll experience resistance to change.

DEVELOPING A VALUE STREAM MAPPING CHARTER

The degree of value stream mapping success is highly dependent on the amount of up-front planning that goes into it, which is most effectively and efficiently reflected in a charter. The charter serves a fourfold purpose: planning, communicating, aligning, and building consensus.

We use variations of the charter shown in Figure 2.2, which includes brief descriptions of the content for each cell. Blank versions of the charter are available for download at www.vsmbook.com. If you prefer to create your own or use a standard charter that your organization has already adopted, we recommend that you include the elements we've included in our charter, described in the following sections.

Scope

This section defines the parameters of the mapping activity. A clearly defined scope helps ensure that the right people are included on the team and reduces the risk that the team will spend valuable time during the activity agreeing on what they should focus on. The goal

FIGURE 2.2 Value stream mapping charter

Value Stream Mapping Charter

Scope

Value Stream	Value stream being improved
Specific Conditions	What circumstances are included and excluded? (e.g., type of customer, geographic location, etc.)
Demand Rate	How many times is this done per wk, qtr, mo, or yr?
Trigger	What initiates the process?
First Step	Task on first process block
Last Step	Task on last process block
Boundaries & Limitations	What is the team NOT authorized to change?
Improvement Time Frame	Typically 3-6 months

Accountable Parties

Executive Sponsor	Required: typically VP or C-level
Value Stream Champion	If needed—often director or manager level
Facilitator	Required: skilled, objective person leading the activity
Logistics Coordinator	Not always needed
Briefing Attendees	List the people that are required to attend the briefings (**) and those whose attendance is optional (*). ** required *optional

Logistics

Event Dates & Times	3 days typically; consecutive is best; 6 hrs per day minimum; 7 or 8 hrs is best
Base-camp Location	On-site, ample wall space, quiet/private location
Meals Provided	Always a nice touch; keeps the team from wandering
Briefing Dates & Times	Aids in consensus building and organizational learning. Typically the last hour of the day.

Mapping Team

	Function	Name	Contact Information
1	Leadership-heavy		
2			
3			
4			
5			
6			
7			
8			
9			
10			

On-Call Support

	Function	Name	Contact Information
1	SMEs that may not be needed full time		
2			
3			
4			

Agreement

Executive Sponsor	Value Stream Champion	Facilitator
Signature:	Signature:	Signature:
Date:	Date:	Date:

Current State Problems & Business Needs

	What's driving the need for improvement?
1	
2	
3	
4	
5	

Measurable Target Condition

1	Reduce <defined metric> from X to Y (Z% improvement).
2	Increase <defined metric> from X to Y (Z% improvement).
3	
4	
5	

Benefits to Customers

	How will internal and / or external customers benefit as a result of improvements to the VS?
1	
2	
3	
4	
5	

Benefits to Business

	What other benefits will the business or internal customers realize as a result of improvements to the VSM?
1	
2	
3	
4	

is to prepare your mapping team so that it's extremely clear about its mission long before it gathers for the first day of the activity. The information we typically include is outlined below.

Value Stream

Here, you describe the value stream to be mapped, whether a *full customer-facing value stream* (e.g., software development, new client implementation, film production, mortgage application, litigation, emergency department patient care, new facility construction, and so on), a *value stream segment* (a portion of a larger value stream), or a *value-enabling (support) value stream* that doesn't provide a good or service directly to an external customer. Purchasing is an example of a function that can be either a value stream segment (e.g., when buying material and supplies in the preproduction phase of a production value stream) or a support value stream (e.g., when buying office equipment or software applications that support the provision of value). The Appendices include examples of all three types of value streams: Appendices B, D, and E are examples of full value streams, Appendix C is a support value stream, and Appendix F is a value stream segment.

Specific Conditions

Here, you include the specific set of conditions that you're including or excluding in the mapping activity—at least for the current state portion. While scoping is always important, proper scoping is even more critical when value stream mapping in office, service, and knowledge work environments, where significant process variation often exists within a single product family. (As we mentioned in Chapter 1, product families include goods and services that pass through common processes.)

To work through the current state mapping activity as quickly as possible, and yet create the environment for deep understanding to occur, it's helpful to narrow your scope and have the mapping team consider a very specific set of conditions for the current state. Otherwise, you risk spending significant time trying to understand all of the possible variations and not getting to the important work of understanding how the work flows, where the disconnects are, and so on.

For example, take the order fulfillment value stream. In many organizations, orders follow extremely different paths depending on the type of order. Figure 2.3 shows how the scope for mapping an order fulfillment value stream segment can be appropriately narrowed. The variants with thick borders reflect the specific conditions that a team focused on as it created the current state.

FIGURE 2.3 Proper scoping is needed to successfully map the current state.

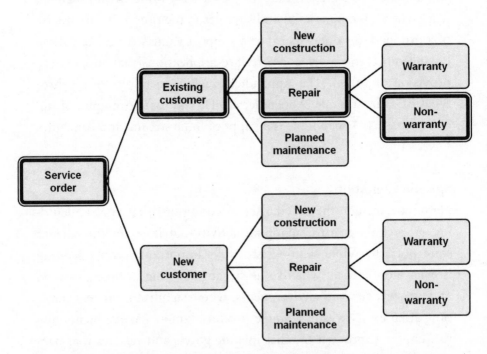

Or you may have a business need to improve an outpatient imaging value stream. There may be significant variation in the work depending on whether the patient is having an MRI, CT scan, mammogram, or x-ray. In preparing the charter, you may decide to focus solely on CT scans to create the current state value stream map (VSM), based on defined criteria (e.g., highest volume, highest margin, most problematic, etc.). You'll see current and future state value stream maps for this example in Appendix B.

Here's the interesting thing that we see time and time again: in many cases, the specific conditions being mapped may end up representing 25 percent or less of the total volume of work in that value stream (e.g., pediatric appointments may account for only 20 percent of all visits to a medical clinic; only 15 percent of engineering drawings may need to go through a complex review process). Yet teams often find that the future state design applies to 75 percent or more of the variation in the value stream. Value stream mapping often demonstrates that, at a macro level, there isn't as much variation as it "feels" like there is.*

Simplifying one's thinking about work flow can be highly unifying, a necessary condition for executing consensus-driven improvement.† When people see that there isn't as much substantive variation at a macro level as it seems at a micro level, it becomes easier to address complexity without introducing unnecessary complication. We regularly find that similar performance issues exist, regardless of the specific type of work flowing through the value stream. Don't be afraid to narrow your scope beyond your comfort level. Again, in nearly every case we've encountered, once the team members design a future state for the narrow set of conditions they've established for the current state value stream map, they find that the future state map applies to a far broader set of conditions.

---

*In Chapter 3, you'll learn how to address the process variation that still may exist even within a narrowly defined scope.

†*Consensus*, used throughout this book, means that a team fully *commits* to a decision, plan, or action, even if not all parties fully *agree* with the decision, plan, or action.

Demand Rate

This is the volume of incoming work per day, week, month, or year. In some office and service environments, this seemingly basic data point can be surprisingly difficult to obtain. But it's critical information that you must have. It's impossible to truly understand current state performance without knowing the volume and types of work flowing through a system. And it's difficult to design flow and pull in a system if you don't know the quantity of work the system needs to accommodate. It's also critical that you know the degree to which there's variation in demand: does work arrive in regular, predictable cycles, or is it erratic? Combining historical data (an indicator of future patterns) with real-time market "intel" is the best way to determine future patterns.

Trigger

This is the thought or action that initiates work flowing through the value stream. It can be a customer decision, an external occurrence of some sort, a scheduled activity, or some other action. Examples of triggers include a customer submitting a purchase order, a person resigning, a patient arriving, a plaintiff filing a lawsuit, and so on.

First Step, Last Step

We refer to the first step and last step as the "fence posts" between which the team will focus its attention. While there are occasional situations that call for adjusting the fence posts during the mapping activity itself, you want to become as clear as possible up front because team formation is dependent upon the processes that will be included in the value stream map. Defining the scope up front also reduces the risk of "scope creep" during the activity. When listing the first and last steps for the processes that will be included in the map, we recommend that you use a verb-plus-noun format to reflect the process in its active form—for example, "enter order" (instead of "order entry"), "register patient" (instead of "patient registration"), and so on.

Boundaries and Limitations

This section houses the boundaries and limitations the team needs to operate within, if any. Here you want to include decisions and actions that the team is *not* authorized to take. They could be financial, systems related, customer or market specific, staff or organizational in nature, or physical. Examples we've encountered include not allowing complex IT modifications due to imminent software upgrades; a stated cap on spending; no staffing increases; and no changes to corporate policies that the organization isn't prepared to address within the value stream improvement window (e.g., the value stream mapping activity may take place within a subsidiary or branch location that has limited ability to affect corporate policies within the transformation time frame). While the mapping team should surface any and all barriers to flow or to delivering value—and should address those discoveries during the briefings and in summary reports distributed to leadership—it's also important to be pragmatic, avoid creating an atmosphere of unrealistic expectations, and recognize constraints that can't be addressed within the defined time frame.

Improvement Time Frame

This is the defined time frame for executing improvements to realize the future state design. You need to decide whether the mapping team should design a future state that it intends to fully realize within 90 days, six months, or one year, for example. In some cases, a firm deadline for improvement is based on a time-sensitive business need (e.g., an acquisition or new product launch). In other cases, you may want to wait until the future state design is completed and then project how much time the organization will need to make a defined set of improvements, based on the organization's ability to absorb change.

Our preferred way of operating is to have a defined time period and scale the future state design to fit within that frame. We typically advise organizations to take a shorter-term approach, such as three to six months, to drive a bias to action. Longer-term views are at greater risk of stalling due to distractions, shifting leadership priorities, and changing conditions in technology, the marketplace, the regulatory environment, and so on. That said, aggressive shorter-term views aren't for everyone. We occasionally work with clients on both larger-scale and slower-paced value stream transformations.

Current State Problems and Business Needs

Part of the value of a well-crafted and well-socialized charter is the alignment you can achieve up, down, and across an organization about the problems the organization faces and why improvement is needed. Clarity is a significant lever for building consensus and driving change.

Avoid the temptation to rush through this section. Taking the time to identify, gain consensus around, and succinctly communicate the top two to five reasons for tackling improvement across an entire value stream will save you significant time during and after the mapping activity because you won't need to sell people on the need for change. The problems and needs could be financial, operational, market related, compliance related, people related, or any combination thereof. When possible, include data to scale the problem and provide context.

Measurable Target Condition

This section of the charter reflects how aggressively you plan to improve. You'll notice that, in the value stream mapping charter in Figure 2.2, we suggest that you include not only the raw numbers for the current and future state (from X to Y), but also the percentage of improvement that they represent. This is particularly important in circumstances in which the raw numbers seemingly reflect only minor improvement and yet are significant on a percentage basis. For example, improving overall quality from 5 percent to 15 percent may seem insufficient to declare a victory. Yet those numbers represent a 200 percent improvement. The opposite is true as well. Shaving two weeks from the lead time may seem significant—and it is if the current state lead time is four weeks (50 percent improvement). But in the case of a complex value stream with a 12-month lead time, shaving two weeks represents less than a 4 percent gain and may not be sufficient for the business needs at hand.

In those cases where the baseline (current state) metrics that you'll use to measure progress aren't known at the time you're creating the charter, you can begin by stating the percentage improvement you seek and then include the raw numbers once you obtain the baseline information.

Benefits to Customers and Benefits to Business

Similar to the reasons for clearly articulating the drivers behind studying and improving a particular value stream, listing two to five direct and collateral (indirect) benefits of value stream improvement to both the organization and its customers is another way to pave the way for reduced resistance to change, accelerate execution of improvements, and deepen "big picture" understanding from the front lines to senior leaders. Communicating this information also enables upfront consensus building across the leadership team, which creates the environment for greater focus and support when the transformation plan is being executed. This section also provides the opportunity to articulate benefits that may be more difficult to measure, such as reduced stress, improved working relationships, and so on.

Accountable Parties

For the greatest success with value stream improvement, you need designated people serving in defined roles with clear responsibilities. At least two of the parties described in the next section are required: the executive sponsor and facilitator. The others depend on many factors, such as organization size, structure, and maturity, whether the activity's being facilitated by an external facilitator, and so on.

Executive Sponsor

The executive sponsor is typically a vice president, plant or general manager, or C-level leader who's ultimately accountable for the results. Ideally, this required role is filled by a person who oversees the entire value stream. But in many organizations, no one person oversees all functions that make up a value stream until you reach the president or CEO level. In small organizations, the president or CEO is often the best person to serve as the executive sponsor. In larger organizations, the executive sponsor is typically the senior leader with the greatest degree of "skin in the game." In rare cases, the executive sponsor is a more minor player in the value stream, but he or she carries stronger influence and enthusiasm for improvement than the executive who oversees the areas with the greatest degree of involvement in the value stream. The executive sponsor may or may not be on the team. At a minimum, the executive sponsor should be actively engaged in the development of the charter, address the team during the kickoff, attend the briefings, and monitor progress on the transformation plan.

Value Stream Champion

Ideally, the value stream champion is someone who's accountable for performance of the entire value stream and, in a hierarchical organization, is a step or two closer to the work than the executive sponsor. In organizations without this designated role, the value stream champion may be a director or manager who oversees a significant portion of the value stream. With the exception of smaller value streams, this person is nearly always on the mapping team.

Less critical value streams, such as new vendor processing, or smaller value stream segments, such as month-end close in finance, may not require senior leadership's direct involvement. The key to deciding is the degree of likelihood that the future state design will involve strategic decisions that only a senior leader is authorized to make, the level of authority lower levels carry, how critical the value stream is, and organizational maturity. If the value stream will require less dramatic improvements, seasoned middle managers who carry greater responsibility may be capable of driving value stream improvement.

Facilitator

Selecting an appropriate facilitator is arguably one of the key success factors in value stream mapping. The facilitator serves varied roles that range from teacher to timekeeper and from skilled change agent to provocateur. Strong facilitators are also comfortable with conflict, possess strong listening skills, and are equally proficient at leading a team through the discovery, design, and planning phases of the mapping activity. They understand organizational dynamics and the psychology of change and are skilled at challenging paradigms in a respectful and supportive way. A good facilitator can also maneuver effectively in various environments, and has the ability to connect quickly and communicate easily with people at all levels of the organization. To maintain objectivity, the facilitator should neither oversee nor work in any part of the value stream being transformed.

Logistics Coordinator

This person is responsible for booking the room that serves as base camp for the mapping team, ordering food, gathering supplies (4- by 6-inch and smaller Post-its, 36-inch-wide mapping paper, scissors, tape or pushpins, and markers), setting up e-connectivity if needed, and so on. Internal facilitators often double as the logistics coordinator.

Briefing Attendees

Daily briefings are a way to align the organization around change and engage relevant parties who aren't on the mapping team. Depending on the organization's experience with value stream mapping, the briefings can also serve as effective sales and learning activities. In this case, you may want to invite a larger stakeholder audience to attend. The briefings are also important steps in gaining organization-wide support and leadership alignment around impending change. Ideally, all of the relevant leaders are on the mapping team itself, but, with a target team size of 5 to 7 members—and in no case more than 10 members (this is discussed in more detail later in this chapter)—this isn't always possible. It's also important to introduce value stream mapping and systems thinking to the leaders in various support functions such as human resources, finance, and information technology. In many cases, you'll need to engage the support areas in making improvement. It's better that they "grow" with the process rather than being brought in cold when you need to achieve rapid consensus and commitment to provide resources. In the following section, we'll go into greater detail about the purpose, format, and logistics around these briefings.

Logistics

Your charter should include logistics information such as the dates and times for the mapping activity, the location of the "base camp" from which the mapping team will operate when they're not walking the value stream (described in Chapter 3), whether meals will be provided, and the dates and times for the briefings mentioned above.

For the team's base camp, select a room that has ample wall space for the 36-inch-wide paper you'll use for mapping. You should also select a room that can comfortably accommodate the additional people who will attend the briefings.

We strongly recommend that you hold the mapping activity on-site rather than at a hotel or conference center. First, the team needs easy access to the value stream's processes and the people who perform them. Second, while it's tempting to believe that the team will have greater focus if they're sequestered away from the workplace, organizations need to develop the ability to focus on key activities while operating in the normal work environment. Remember, well-executed value stream activities achieve more than the defined target conditions. They also help replace counterproductive organizational habits with more effective ways of operating.

Especially in organizations new to value stream mapping, we recommend that you hold periodic briefings as mentioned earlier. In a three-phase mapping activity, the briefings serve three different purposes. At the end of Phase 1, the team members share the current state value stream map and the deep understanding they've gained. While it is often sobering for leadership to confront the reality about the existing system through which work flows, it's an important step toward organization-wide learning and alignment, and it helps establish a sense of urgency around value stream improvement. Remember that, with the exception of the mapping team, the current state briefing is often the first time any one person in the organization has been exposed to how work passes through the entire system and has seen the disconnects and dysfunction in such a clear way. Spreading understanding about the current state to people beyond the mapping team reduces organizational resistance to change down the road. When a critical mass of people agree, "Yes, this is how we operate," it's far more difficult to say, "We don't need to change." The briefing is also an effective venue for correcting assumptions and misperceptions about value stream performance, roles and responsibilities, and customer requirements, to name a few.

Holding periodic briefings—*and having all relevant parties in attendance*—is an even more critical step after the future state is designed (Phase 2). The second briefing provides an efficient way to gain consensus around the future state design that would otherwise require a "sales cycle" after the future state value stream design is complete. We've seen sales cycles delay the start of improvement by months and, in many cases, halt improvement altogether. What a waste of time, money, and emotional energy to have 5 to 10 highly paid leaders spend three days learning about how the organization truly functions and designing system-wide improvements only to have someone else in the organization nix or indefinitely stall the entire project!

A third and final briefing that includes a review of the value stream transformation plan (Phase 3) serves multiple purposes as well. First, it demonstrates effective planning practices. The final briefing serves as an excellent model for gaining commitment to highly effective action plans that are neither too rigid to incorporate real-time discoveries nor too loose to create the type of momentum, accountability, and focus that's needed in the face of tempting distractions. You're a step ahead when you conclude the mapping activity with leaders from across the organization, show them how the team intends to make progress, and obtain their public commitment to support the plan.

For all of these reasons, it's critical that you consider leadership team availability when selecting dates for mapping. We've seen too many value stream mapping activities fail because a key leader was on vacation and, therefore, didn't benefit from the real-time learning, debate, and consensus building that makes for a smoother transformation process down the road. Remember, transforming a value stream often produces a fair amount of organizational disruption. Leaders need time to grow comfortable with planned improvement, prepare their teams for change, and free resources to support the transformation activities.

A final logistics detail that's not included on the charter is preparing to walk the value stream. This activity is described in Chapter 3, and it requires up-front planning. The work areas need to be prepared and, if special access badges or permissions are needed, approvals obtained in advance.

Mapping Team

Your charter should also include a list of the mapping participants. Generally speaking, the smaller the team, the more effective the results—as long as all functions in the value stream are represented. Five to seven participants, representing all the functions that play a significant role in the process, are best. For value streams that are IT intensive, we recommend that you include a systems subject-matter expert on the team. In no case should the team have more than 10 people. Having more than 10 people on the team creates logistics challenges with walking the value stream, enabling everyone to actively participate in the activity, and facilitating effectively. It also introduces greater risk of experiencing resistance to change and time management issues, which often occurs when you have too many "cooks in the kitchen." If the number of people needed to represent all key functions across the value stream exceeds 10, you should scope the value stream more narrowly or hold longer briefings and invite those leaders to air any concerns or future state design ideas.

If the executive sponsor or value stream champion is on the team, he or she should be listed both in the Accountable Parties section and as a team member. The facilitator is not listed as part of the team.

The team should be heavily biased with leadership (typically managers and above) who can influence and authorize the type of future state improvements that will be needed to truly transform the value stream. We've facilitated value stream mapping activities where the entire team was composed of vice presidents and C-level leaders. In these cases, the future state design is often far better suited to achieve the business goals than it is when lower-level leaders are on the mapping team. The challenge is getting senior leaders to commit to a sequestered team activity over three consecutive days.

While senior leaders don't necessarily know the details about how the value stream currently performs, pre-event data gathering and the value stream walk (described in Chapter 3) fill that need. If you fill the team with lower-level leaders who know the details but can't authorize transformational improvements, you risk introducing delays into the improvement process as you sell the need for the specific countermeasures* the team has in mind.

A final reason for biasing the team with senior leaders is that the more senior the leaders, the better able they are to understand "the big picture," which can lead to more innovative (and, therefore, often more disruptive) suggestions. Remember, we're not talking about process-level mapping where a team is designing tactical improvements. That type of work is often a necessary follow-on activity after value stream mapping, but improving at a macro level often requires bold thinking. Our advice regarding team composition is to "go as high as you can and accept as low as you need to," articulating team composition benefits and risks along the way. Convincing leaders that they need to give up three days isn't an easy sell, but by clearly identifying the business needs and why their participation is important, you can increase their understanding of why their involvement is a key success factor.

On-Call Support

On-call support is reserved for those parties who either play a very minor role in the value stream or provide indirect support to one or more areas in the value stream. These leaders are often required for the briefings but are not needed full-time on the team. They do, however, need to be immediately available if the team needs them, so they shouldn't fill their calendars with daylong commitments that can't be interrupted. Be careful with this one. It's tempting to put time-constrained leaders or subject-matter experts on call when they need to be full-time team members.

---

*We prefer the term *countermeasures* over *solutions* because *solution* often implies a degree of permanence that's counter to establishing a continuous improvement mindset.

Agreement

Depending on your organization's culture and maturity, you may or may not need a signature area on your charter to communicate agreement with and commitment to the mapping activity and subsequent value stream transformation. If you find it helpful, we recommend you include signatures from the executive sponsor, value stream champion, and facilitator.

SOCIALIZING THE VALUE STREAM MAPPING CHARTER

We prefer the term *socializing* to *communicating* because it indicates that more is needed than merely e-mailing the charter around the company. Charter socialization is an important step in shaping the transformation. It lays the groundwork for successful execution of improvements and reduces the risk of obstacles that may otherwise arise months after the actual mapping activity.

It's critical that you engage three groups in understanding the charter: (1) affected leadership; (2) the mapping team members; and (3) the workers in the areas that will be included in the value stream walk to understand the current state (described in Chapter 3). If the people who work the value stream are going to be called upon to demonstrate work tasks, they need to be fully aware of the why, what, how, and when of value stream mapping. Frontline workers may also need to be prepped for talking with a level of leadership with which they may not be used to interacting. A safe environment for honest exchanges must be established, or the truth around the current state may be shrouded in fear.

As we mentioned in Chapter 1, value stream improvement should be closely tied to an organization's defined business needs and aligned with the organizational purpose and strategic direction.

If this is the case, you should have very little disagreement across the leadership team about value stream improvement being a significant priority. But leadership teams new to value stream mapping still need to understand the process, weigh in on scope, agree that value stream improvement is a high priority, and understand how executing the future state design will be accomplished.

Organizations that skip this vital step of socializing the charter with leadership (through conversation, not merely as an e-mail attachment) often have to navigate through and around obstacles that would otherwise not exist. It's far better to have difficult conversations and gain leadership commitment to the activity up front instead of taking the risk that it will occur during the mapping activity itself or that the team will have to gain commitment after the future state is already designed.

In one of the worst cases we've seen, an organization failed to involve its full leadership team in the development and socialization of the charter. At the end of the second day of a three-day value stream mapping activity, a vice president over one of the functional areas that played a key role in the value stream announced that the team was designing to the "wrong" target condition and was not authorized to make the key improvements that the future state design depended on. The ensuing debate revealed significant disagreement between three leaders that the planning team should have discovered and worked through as the charter was being developed. Unfortunately, the leaders weren't able to reconcile their differing viewpoints that day, so the team—which included two key suppliers and two employees who had been flown in from Europe and the Middle East—did what it could to complete an altered future state design and prepare a transformation plan. The unfortunate outcomes from not involving a broader set of leaders in the planning stage and/or properly socializing the charter resulted in a transformation plan that was never fully executed. It was an expensive mistake and, to the team, a demoralizing miss.

One final point: charter formation is an iterative process. As you begin scoping, defining objectives, forming the team, and planning the logistics, new information often surfaces that alters previous decisions. To improve the odds for mapping success, exercise humility and adopt an inclusive process for charter development. Top-down mandates from an executive sponsor or a leader over a specific functional area are the antithesis of the type of consensus building that accelerates improvement. While the charter should be finalized before the mapping activity, it sometimes requires modification as it's being socialized and greater insights are obtained.

COLLECTING DATA

The data you need to collect up front is largely dependent on the nature of the value stream being mapped, improvement drivers, and defined target conditions. One piece of data that we, as facilitators, consistently ask for up front is current and forecasted customer demand (incoming work volume or number of requests) for the next one to two years so that the future state design accommodates increased growth or shrinkage. We also ask for quality reports that quantify internal or external issues (if the data exists). For data-rich, high-volume processes, it may be helpful to collect data around demand patterns, service levels, lead times, and productivity, but make sure you don't turn this into a data collection exercise and succumb to analysis paralysis. Nor should up-front data supplant what the mapping team directly observes during the value stream walks.

Another preparation step we typically take—usually very early in the planning process—is to walk or talk through the value stream so that we can estimate how much time to allot for walking the value stream and how "big" the map will likely be. Having a rough idea about the process blocks the map may include is also helpful for understanding which functions need to be included when socializing the charter, and for preparing workers for the value stream walk. Laying out the likely process blocks also ensures that all relevant functions are represented on the mapping team.

In some cases when we can't walk the full value stream due to physical constraints, virtual working environments, or secured areas, we also ask for the quantity of work-in-process (queued work) at each process throughout the value stream. We generally wait until the mapping activity itself to collect all other data so that the entire team benefits from the process of deciding what's relevant and experiencing how difficult collecting real-time data may be. After all, data gaps are important discoveries!

Once you've set the stage for success by proper planning, you're ready for the big day: Phase 1 of the mapping activity, the subject of Chapter 3.

3

Understanding the Current State

Gaining a deep understanding of current state value stream performance is a vital step in designing and making improvement. After all, how can you improve work flow if you don't understand how the work is being performed today? All too often, well-intentioned people rush to "solutions," resulting in short-term fixes and the risk of making matters even worse. Lacking clarity about the current state or operating with incomplete facts, assumptions, and incorrect information contributes to persistent and recurring problems.

The current state value stream map enables everyone in the organization to see the truth about how the value stream is performing. When the current state value stream map is socialized across the organization and people come together and agree that, yes, this is how we currently operate, the map has begun to achieve a larger purpose: consensus building to accelerate improvement. It bears repeating: this is where many have shortchanged value stream mapping; used properly, it serves a much larger mission than merely making improvement. While the results from current state mapping can be sobering (it's not always easy confronting the truth in such a visible and data-driven way), they're extremely powerful for achieving a collective understanding and consensus around problems. Improvement design and implementation moves more quickly and is met with less resistance when it's based on what is actually occurring, as opposed to differing perceptions of or opinions about what is occurring.

The current state value stream map is a visual storyboard that shows how the work currently gets done. It represents how work flows, who does the work, and how the value stream is performing *on the day the map is created*. Members of mapping teams often argue that "what we are seeing today is not normal" and want to map the process the way it should perform, how it used to perform, or how it sometimes performs. We have observed that, when you ask people to describe a specific process in a value stream, there are at least four different versions: how managers believe it operates, how it's supposed to operate (i.e., the written procedure, if one exists), how it really operates, and how it could operate. The purpose of current state value stream mapping is to get an understanding of how work is *actually* being performed in *today's* environment. Because the current state map represents a snapshot in time, the observations the team makes and the metrics it collects reflect value stream performance on that specific day. For value streams with high variation in incoming work volume, quality of inputs, accumulation of work-in-process (WIP), or the time it takes to complete the work, the team should make a note of the variation, but the map should reflect the value stream *as it existed on the day in which it was mapped.**

ACTIVITY KICKOFF

On the first day of the mapping activity, the facilitator should prepare the "base camp" conference or meeting room by hanging 36-inch-wide paper on the wall upon which the mapping team will construct

---

*In value streams with high variation, it may be helpful to revisit the value stream on a different day to explore how it operates in different conditions.

the map using four- by six-inch Post-its*. Base the paper length on the facilitator's prework to understand the value stream.

After the mapping team has arrived, we recommend that you kick off the event with team introductions, even if the team members all know one another. Identifying each of their roles in the value stream begins to highlight the interconnected nature of the work and the process of shifting mindsets from siloed thinking to holistic thinking. You may also include a suggestion that, as team members are introducing themselves and the functions they represent, they specify who their external or internal suppliers and customers are, again to highlight the interconnectedness of the value stream components. It's also helpful to ask each participant to share his or her expectations and/or concerns about the three-day mapping activity. If team members' expectations are not in line with the approved charter, that disconnect should be discussed before moving forward. But, with a properly socialized charter, the chance of discovering disconnects at this stage should be virtually eliminated.

After introductions, the executive sponsor should address the team—in person, if possible—to reiterate the business drivers for improving the value stream, his or her expectations for the mapping activity, and his or her faith in the team to achieve the measurable conditions outlined in the charter.

Either the executive sponsor or the value stream champion should also review the charter with the team once again so that the team is clear about the scope and its mission. Even if the charter has been broadly socialized, reviewing it again at the start of the mapping activity reinforces the team's shared mission, which can be helpful especially during future state design when discomfort with change may rear its head. Having the executive sponsor or value stream champion review the charter during the kickoff also serves as a clear message that the charter is the team's, not the facilitator's, and that the mapping activity outcomes are owned by the team, not the facilitator.

---

*Some teams prefer to draw the map directly on the 36-inch-wide paper, on 11" × 17" paper, or on a whiteboard.

The charter should not be open for debate at this stage of the process. Unless new information has surfaced, the team should commit to the scope and measurable targets that were established during the planning phase. This should not be the last time the team reviews the charter, however. When we facilitate, we typically revisit the charter several times during the activity to reinforce points, rechannel the team members' energy, and get the team back on track if it loses focus.

At this point, the executive sponsor and/or value stream champion turns the activity over to the facilitator, who, after a brief introduction, reviews a notional agenda for the activity, and seeks consensus around the "rules of engagement" that will create the greatest degree of success (see sidebar for a sample of the rules we often use). We use the term *notional* for the agenda because, while facilitators should have a solid plan for the activity, there needs to be a little flex built in to allow for the varying lengths of time the current state discovery process and future state design can take.

If the team hasn't been exposed to Lean thinking, PDSA, and value stream basics, the facilitator should provide a brief overview. However, as we mentioned in Chapter 2, it's preferable that the overview occur prior to the activity so that you don't eat into the time the team needs for mapping. You want to begin mapping as quickly in the day as possible.

Rules of Engagement for Improvement Activities

We typically work with our clients to select the rules of engagement that match the culture and the conditions under which we'll be working. These are the most common "rules" we use. We gain the team's agreement with the rules during the kickoff, modifying as needed. We often use a three-knock rule: anyone can knock three times on the table if he or she feels a rule is being violated, and the team will address it. Posting the rules in a visible place in the base camp is an effective way to minimize straying from the rules.

- The activity begins and ends on time; being on time is critical.
- No interruptions; the team stays 100 percent committed and focused.
- All wireless devices on silent mode or off. No vibration.
- Laptops closed.
- No e-mail, IMs, or texts except during breaks or to obtain information directly relevant to the activity.
- Rank has no privilege.
- Finger-pointing and blame have no place.
- Seek the wisdom of ten versus the knowledge of one.
- Use creativity over capital; mind over money.
- Think externally. Eliminate siloed and "us" versus "them" thinking.
- No silent objectors.
- Respectful disagreement is encouraged; it's not acceptable to be disagreeable.
- What's said in the room stays in the room until a plan for appropriate messaging has been defined.
- Eliminate "can't" and "No, because . . ." from your vocabulary. Adopt a "Yes, if . . ." mindset.
- Eliminate "this is the way we've always done it" thinking.
- Ask "why?" "why not?" and "what if?"
- One conversation at a time; avoid talking over each other.
- Be bold.

After the kickoff, the team is ready to get started. They should begin by labeling the 36-inch-wide paper in the upper right-hand corner. Typical information includes the value stream name, "current state," the included and/or excluded conditions, customer demand (work volume), the names of the sponsor and mapping team members, and the date.

Before we get into the process for creating the current state value stream map, we want to introduce you to an important part of the mapping process that is often foreign to mapping teams in office and service environments: walking the value stream.

VALUE STREAM WALKS

A critical step in creating the current state map is physically walking the value stream, also known as "going to the gemba." *Gemba* is a Japanese term that means "the real place, where the work is actually done."* By going to the gemba, the team is able to observe the work, talk to the workers in their environment, and learn about obstacles to flow firsthand, thereby grasping the current condition more fully. People are typically more comfortable talking with others in their own environment; being asked to come to a conference room to help a leadership-heavy team evaluate work flow can evoke understandable anxiety and make them feel like they are on a witness stand. It is much more effective to go to them.

Even if the entire value stream is performed in cubicles or enclosed offices, you typically get a far deeper understanding by actually walking the process. When the mapping team members walk the process they can experience the physical conditions within which a value stream

---

*Gemba can also be spelled with an *n*: genba. While we have chosen to use the Romanized and more commonly used version with an *m*, according to *hiragana* (a Japanese syllabary), *n* is actually a more correct translation. In this book we use "going to the gemba" and "value stream walk" interchangeably.

operates. We've had many mapping teams see, feel, hear, and sometime even smell current state conditions that needed to be improved that they never would have experienced if they constructed the current state value stream map solely from a conference room. Also, only by going to the gemba can you appreciate the physical separation and isolation that may exist between upstream supplier and downstream customer, and observe whether visual management exists.

A final reason to perform value stream walks is to break through "inattentional blindness" that may exist when people have grown used to specific working conditions.* When "outside eyes"—people who don't live the process—intentionally and directly study a work environment, they can often see causes for performance problems that would otherwise go undetected.

For a value stream walk to be truly effective, you need to properly prepare the workforce in the area being visited so employees understand the objectives and spirit (understanding, not judgment) in which the walk will be conducted. The workers need to understand that the focus is on work systems design, not individuals' performance. To speak candidly, they must be free of fear. We often emphasize that we want to know what is really happening, so there is no need to be afraid to tell us everything, and that the exercise is based on a need to understand, not an interest in being punitive. After all, if the team doesn't understand where the breakdowns are, how can they learn where the countermeasures need to be focused? For example, we've facilitated a number of value stream mapping activities during which workers revealed noncompliant activities that caught leadership off guard but were critical to learn and were quickly resolved. Without a high degree of trust, these revelations might not have been made. As we mentioned in Chapter 2,

---

*Inattentional blindness, also known as perceptual blindness, is the failure to notice an unexpected stimulus in one's field of vision when other attention-demanding tasks are being performed. It often occurs when there are excessive stimuli in one's environment. For more information, see http://en.wikipedia.org/wiki/Inattentional_blindness.

it's critical to communicate thoroughly with the people the team will be visiting and provide opportunities for questions to properly quell the anxiety that could result in a subpar walk.

Since we strongly recommend that you limit your mapping team to 10 people (remember, fewer is better), and the team is primarily composed of leaders, going to the gemba is an effective way to involve those who best understand what is actually happening within the value stream: the workers themselves. This inclusion pays significant dividends by spreading organizational learning, demonstrating leadership engagement, gaining consensus, and showing respect. It carries other benefits as well. Walking the value stream begins to replace less effective leadership habits of making decisions from offices with "go and see" behaviors, which builds stronger relationships between leadership and the front lines and results in higher quality decisions.

There are times when walking all or part of the value stream may be physically impossible, such as when a portion of the value stream resides in a remote or secured location, or when walking the value stream would be excessively intrusive. For example, in some financial services and software development firms, a significant portion of the value stream may be performed in another country. In this case, you can bring the gemba to the mapping team via online screen sharing, videoconferencing, FaceTime (on Apple devices), and other virtual learning and communication methods. Even if you can't walk the entire value stream, we recommend that you walk the portion of the value stream that's physically accessible.

The logistics of walking the value stream require up-front planning and high levels of sensitivity to the environment. In some environments, the team may need to be extremely discreet—for example, in patient care areas, environments with highly confidential information, or service centers where customers are physically present. If special permission is needed to access a secured area, those arrangements should be made during the planning phase.

For the deepest understanding about the current state, we recommend that the mapping team walk the value stream twice on the
same day. We have found that seeing the value stream in action a
second time allows the team to learn more deeply. Team members
nearly always make additional discoveries during the second walk.
Walking the value stream twice—and, as you'll see in the following
sections, having different objectives for each walk—also makes for
a less overwhelming process for beginning value stream mapping
teams. Seasoned value stream mapping teams may choose to accomplish the missions for both walks in a single walk.

You may choose to walk the value stream from the first to the
last process within the scope you've defined, or you may choose to
walk the value stream in reverse, from the last process to your starting point. There are several advantages to walking the value stream
in the reverse order from how work typically flows. First, it provides
a different perspective that requires more focused attention. Like
walking backward, eating with your less dominant hand, or reading
a sentence backward, doing things in reverse gives you a different
experience and requires you to concentrate more deeply. And that
heightened awareness often provides deeper insights into the value
stream design and cultural issues that need to be addressed.

Second, walking the value stream backward helps the mapping
team see the supplier and customer connections more easily. It's easier
to discover the need for higher quality output from an upstream process when you first ask the downstream recipients to describe what
they receive and what they do with it.

Third, it's easier to see the opportunities to design *pull* into a value
stream when viewing it from the receiving end versus the producing
end. Pull is a work management system where upstream suppliers
deliver work to downstream customers only when the downstream
customers are ready to receive it. It's a technique that helps uncover
work flow problems and accelerates resolution when they arise. Most

processes and value streams that haven't been redesigned using a Lean lens operate as push systems; that is, work is pushed from one function or department to the next function or department regardless of whether the receiving entity (the process's customer) has the capacity to do the work. As a result, work often sits idle until the receiving party is able to work on it. For deeper learning about pull versus push, we recommend Lean classics such as *Lean Thinking* (Womack and Jones) and *The Toyota Way* (Liker).

One firm guideline we follow is that the team walks the value stream together. While it may be tempting to break the team into smaller groups—especially in tight work spaces or in environments where you need to minimize disruptions—a significant benefit of walking the value stream is the conversation that occurs as the team observes the work and the work environment, and notes the effects of siloed process management. You lose this richness when the full mapping team isn't together. Another benefit to keeping the team together is that, because the first walk occurs early in the mapping process, the team is still gelling. We've found that breaking members into subgroups can delay this gelling process.*

DOCUMENTING THE CURRENT STATE

Now that you understand the value of and the logistics around going to the gemba, it's time to introduce the five steps to documenting the current state: walking the value stream, laying out the map, walking the value stream a second time, adding details to the map, and summarizing the map.

---

*We aren't suggesting that we want everyone to think alike. On the contrary, a seasoned facilitator will watch out for "groupthink"—especially during the future state design phase—and take steps to ensure that groupthink doesn't take hold. The gelling process we're referring to is more about the early trust building across the team so that team members feel safe speaking their minds freely.

First Walk

During the first walk, the mapping team begins determining how it will depict the value stream in terms of process blocks. As we mentioned in Chapter 1, a value stream is a series of processes that connect together and transform a customer request into a good or service that's delivered to the customer, which completes the request-to-delivery cycle. The first value stream walk focuses on obtaining the most basic information you need for understanding the current state: the sequence of processes that connect together to form the value stream, and the functions that perform the work. For example, a customer service rep may enter an order, an engineer may quote a project, a nurse may administer medication, a software developer may perform validation testing, a police officer may make an arrest, and so on.

Note that each of these processes is typically made up of a series of steps. Recalling Figure 1.1, the granularity of work represented on a value stream map is macro level; the specific steps needed to generate output are irrelevant at this point. Again, this is what differentiates a value stream map from a process map. A process map would include all of the individual actions (steps) required to enter an order, quote a project, administer medication, perform validation testing, or make an arrest, whereas the value stream map looks at the high-level activities that transform a request into some sort of deliverable. Remember, too, that the purpose of value stream mapping is to design a strategic improvement plan that will be executed over a period of time; it's not designed to address problems at a detailed level.

During the first value stream walk, the team talks with the people doing the work to get a high-level understanding of what's being done to transform an input into an output. At this stage, team members collect information that will help them determine how to construct the map—which process blocks will be on the map and in what order. Though they are not yet collecting metrics or identifying barriers to flow, the team should gain clarity about what inputs the worker receives, where they come from, who they pass work on to, and if the work stops at any point. All mapping team members participate in the interview process and take notes. Active participation by all is critical to gain the collective degree of clarity that's needed to design a future state that will perform at the levels desired. However, it can be helpful to designate one person as the primary scribe and another as the timekeeper to keep the team moving.

It's common for mapping team members to make comments such as "I can't believe we do it this way," and "Why don't we . . . ?" As improvement ideas surface during the walks, they should be captured, but the facilitator should discourage the team members from discussing the merits of the ideas right then or getting drawn too deeply into future state discussions. Instead, they should create an "idea list" that they can refer to during the future state design phase.

The team should also avoid using an accusatory or demeaning tone when talking with the value stream workers. Humility and curiosity demonstrate respect for the people and open the lines of communication, whereas a judgmental tone causes workers to behave defensively or shut down, inhibiting the team's ability to gain valuable insights. This is the time for learning, not judging. Some of the most positive and longest-lasting benefits we've seen from value stream mapping have occurred when leadership-based mapping teams have seen the pain that frontline workers experience in a dysfunctional value stream, and have apologized for placing the workers in a system that doesn't allow them to contribute fully.

Leaders are often surprised by the degree of dysfunction that exists across the value stream and are eager to jump to the future state. During the value stream walks, the facilitator may need to slow the team down so that members gain the deep understanding that's needed to create a robust future state and break their habit of prematurely jumping to solutions.

After the initial walk, the team returns to base camp, compares notes, and reaches consensus about the process blocks that will be on the map as well as their sequence.

Map Layout

Once the team returns to base camp, members begin building a rudimentary view of the value stream by placing four- by six-inch Post-its on the mapping paper. This step is similar to building the foundation for a structure or developing the wireframe for a website. The team focuses on the basics—what is done, who does it, and in what order—upon which they'll layer in details down the road.

The Post-it for the customer—whether external as is found in a full value stream or internal (value stream segment or support value stream)—is typically placed in the top center position on the mapping paper. If the value stream involves outside suppliers, we typically place the customer Post-it in the upper right of our maps and the supplier in the upper left, as is found in classic manufacturing value stream maps. But for those value streams with no external suppliers (the majority we've encountered in office and service settings), we place the customer Post-it in the top center position.

Next, the team agrees on the process blocks that will form the value stream. Determining how macro to go takes some practice. You want to make sure that your value stream map isn't so large that it becomes unwieldy, nor so simple that it becomes useless. To aid in targeting the right level of information, we aim for 5 to 15 serial process blocks. If you end up with fewer than five process blocks on your map, you may not have enough detail to make substantive decisions about the future state. Having more than 15 serial process blocks is an indication that either your scope's too broad for a single mapping activity or, more commonly, you are likely inching your way toward a process-level map and may get tangled up in the tactical weeds rather than staying at a strategic level. If you get too far into the weeds, it's also more difficult to see performance gaps. With experience—especially working with a seasoned facilitator—you'll build proficiency in identifying the right level.

Flow is present when work moves from one process to the next in the value stream without interruption or delay. Generally, a new process block is warranted when the work stops flowing. This often occurs with a handoff to a new work area, when work accumulates (a buildup of work-in-process), or when the work is only processed at a predetermined time interval. From a value stream mapping perspective, judging "when the work stops flowing" is relative. Keep in mind the goal of 15 or fewer serial process blocks, and that complex processes that involve many functions could have well over 15 points where the flow stops. In these situations, the team may need to recalibrate its interpretation of "flow." For example, if a work item sits for two hours between two functions in a value stream with an overall lead time of eight weeks, we may decide to combine those two process blocks even though true flow does not exist between them. Again, these decisions become easier with experience.

Once the team members agree on the process blocks, they write a description of the activities in the fewest words possible and in verb-plus-noun format (e.g., test specimen, interview candidates, enter order, create drawing) and the functions that perform them on the Post-its, using only the upper portion of the Post-it, as pictured in Figure 3.1. They should be placed in the proper sequence across the vertical midpoint of the 36-inch-wide paper you've hung on the wall.

Because a value stream map is a macro view of work, it does not typically contain the type of "swim lanes" that are often found on cross-functional process maps. Value stream maps also don't typically include yes/no decision trees that are often found on process flow charts. Remember, each product family has its own value stream.

FIGURE 3.1 Post-it note after the first value stream walk

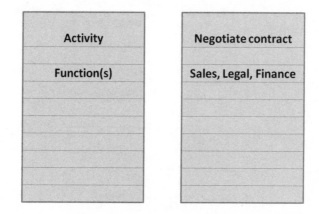

As discussed in Chapter 2, mapping in service, transactional, creative, and analytical environments requires careful scoping around defined conditions. Your current state map should reflect the flow of work for those specific conditions. Since value stream maps are macro level, we usually map what happens 80 percent of the time to reduce variation and focus on improving the majority of the work. This approach often creates greater capacity for an organization to cope with the remaining variation and exceptions.*

As depicted in Figure 3.2, we do occasionally depict a "fork in the road" where, for example, the work proceeds through a particular process some percentage of the time and bypasses that process some percentage of the time. If this is the only deviation in the process, it may not warrant having two separate value stream maps to depict that single point of difference. Remember that value stream mapping is as much art as science—as long as the art doesn't interfere with the science!

---

*Due to any number of business reasons, it may be prudent to focus initially on the 20 percent that are the exceptions. In this case, the charter should clearly define the specific conditions being mapped and the reasons for focusing on the exceptions.

FIGURE 3.2 Acceptable branching on a value stream map

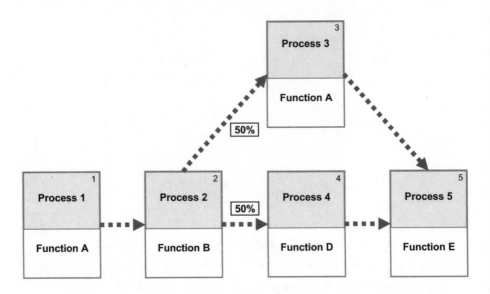

You may also find that the output from one process is passed to two or more functions and is worked on concurrently. We call these parallel processes. In this case, the Post-its are stacked above one another in the same vertical plane. (You'll see an example of this later in Figure 3.12 and again in Appendix D; process blocks 3 and 4 in Figure 3.2 depict branching, not parallel processes.)

Once the team has agreed on what the process blocks are, as well as their sequence, and has placed the Post-its on the mapping paper, it should number the Post-its sequentially. Numbering the Post-its makes it far easier to refer to specific process blocks.

Figure 3.3 depicts an electronic version of a simple value stream map to show how your map should look at this stage.

After the process blocks are numbered, it's time to prepare for the second visit to the gemba. The second walk will focus on collecting relevant information and data to assess current value stream performance and discover both problems and opportunities for improvement.

FIGURE 3.3 Value stream map progressive build: process block placement

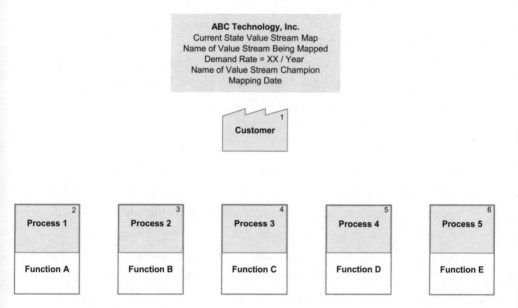

Second Walk

The purpose of the second value stream walk is for the team to gain a deeper understanding about how the value stream currently performs and identify significant barriers to flow. Every value stream has unique characteristics. Therefore, every value stream will require that you assess current state performance based on the specific problems you wish to address and/or opportunities you wish to leverage, the type of work flowing through the system, and the work environment. In most circumstances, grasping the current condition of a value stream targeted for improvement requires that you assess its performance in terms of both time and quality. The team needs to understand the speed at which work progresses from process to process, the hands-on work effort required, and the quality of the process output that moves through the value stream. Obviously, the more delays the work encounters and the poorer the output quality at any point in the value stream, the poorer the overall value stream performance will be.

Key Metrics for Each Process Block

We use three metrics to evaluate the current state of 98 percent of the office and service value streams we've encountered: process time (PT), lead time (LT), and percent complete and accurate (%C&A).

Process Time

Process time (PT)—also referred to as processing time, touch time, work time, and task time*—is the time it takes people to complete the process tasks to transform an input into an output for one unit of work. A unit of work could be one order, one patient, one drawing, one requisition, one meal, and so on. If the work is processed in batches, we typically include the time to process the batch as if the batch only contained one unit.

Typically expressed in minutes or hours, process time represents the hands-on "touch time" to do the work. It also includes "talk time" that may be regularly required to clarify or obtain additional information related to a task (including meetings), as well as "read and think time" if the process involves review or analysis. If both humans and equipment are involved in processing work and the nonhuman work is significant, those times should be identified and recorded separately—e.g., the time it takes for a microbiological culture to grow or an extensive data upload to complete.

Process time does not include waiting or delays. It is the time it would take to do the work *if the process workers could work on one item uninterrupted.* If workers are frequently interrupted or have to ask the upstream supplier for clarification or to add or correct the information supplied, it may be difficult at first for the interviewees to deter-

---

*To minimize confusion, we avoid using the term *cycle time*, as it has several definitions: synonymous with process time, lead time, and the pace or frequency of output, to name a few.

mine the actual process time since it could be the first time they have looked at their work from this perspective. Be patient and guide them.

In office, service, and knowledge work settings, process times often vary according to work complexity, which is one reason we advise that you select a narrow set of conditions to map. When process times vary widely even within a narrow set of conditions, opt for the median rather than the mean so that the measurement more accurately reflects what typically happens.* Process time only includes work that's being done to actively convert input to output. It does *not* include the time that a work item spends in queue before it is reviewed or "touched" for the first time, as it awaits correction or clarification, or as it waits to be passed on to the next person or department in the value stream.

While process time is important, opt for accuracy over precision. Remember, value stream mapping is a strategic look at a series of processes. There's no need for detailed time studies; you only need to know, directionally, more or less how long it takes to do the work. Detailed studies that may be necessary to make tactical improvements are performed as the transformation plan is put through its PDSA paces. The purpose of value stream mapping is to make strategic decisions about the future state.

Process time reflects human effort (and, sometimes, equipment time) and, in the current state, consists of both value-adding and non-value-adding effort. Value-adding effort is work that your *external customer* values and is willing to pay for—or that's a requirement of doing business with the customer. All other expenses and effort are non-value-adding. However, there are two types of non-value-add-

---

*The mean is the arithmetic average of a set of measures: the sum of the measures divided by the number of measures in the set. The median is the midpoint in a set of measures, where half of the measures are above the median and half of the measures are below the median. A mean can be thrown off by a single outlier that rarely occurs, whereas a median will not be affected as dramatically. For example, if the process times for four occurrences of a particular process are 10 minutes, 10 minutes, 20 minutes, and 60 minutes, the mean is 25 minutes, whereas the median is 15 minutes, which is a more accurate reflection of reality.

ing work: necessary and unnecessary.* Necessary non-value-adding work includes activities that an organization believes it must *presently* do to have a viable business. We sometimes refer to this work as value-enabling. In other words, if this work wasn't performed, the organization would be hard-pressed to deliver value. Unnecessary non-value-adding work is true waste: the customer doesn't value it and the business doesn't have to do it to remain a viable enterprise. The goal of value stream transformation is to deliver greater value to one's customers. One means for achieving greater value is to eliminate non-value-adding work—or, in the case of necessary non-value-adding work, reduce it so that it consumes fewer resources.† Value stream mapping helps us identify how to achieve this goal.

Some value stream mapping activities benefit from having the team evaluate each process block to determine if the work being done is primarily value-adding (as viewed by the *external* customer), primarily necessary non-value-adding, or primarily unnecessary non-value-adding, keeping in mind that some process blocks may include all three types of work. Teams newer to Lean and/or value stream mapping often benefit from a brief exercise where they label the process blocks with a "VA" for value-adding or an "N" for necessary non-value-adding. In this case, the facilitator should help the team stay at a macro level and avoid getting into the details of the specific processes represented on the map. More seasoned mapping teams may not need to call out what's obvious to them.

---

*Some organizations may prefer to use the terms *essential* and *nonessential*. In *Lean Thinking*, authors Womack and Jones refer to necessary non-value-adding work as Type One *muda* (waste) and unnecessary non-value-adding work as Type Two *muda*. The Lean community commonly recognizes eight types of waste: overproduction, overprocessing, errors, inventory, waiting, transportation, motion, and underutilization of people (in terms of experience, knowledge, skills, and creativity)—all of which are symptoms of underlying problems. The benefits of categorizing waste include helping people identify the full range of waste that may exist and the countermeasures that address the root cause(s) for the waste. The eight wastes were originally defined in manufacturing, but we have observed these same wastes in *all* environments to varying degrees. Similarly, every example of waste we've seen in office, service, and knowledge work environments has easily fit into one of these eight categories.

†Other goals of value stream mapping are to eliminate *mura* (unevenness) and *muri* (overburden).

Lead Time

Lead time (LT)— also referred to as throughput time, response time, and turnaround time—is the elapsed time from the moment work is made available to an individual, work team, or department until it has been completed and made available to the next person or team in the value stream. Lead time is often expressed in hours, days, or even weeks or months. If incoming work sits in a department's electronic queue for an average of six hours before anyone begins work on it, and then it takes a person an average of 30 minutes (process time) to complete the work, and then it's held for an additional hour before it's passed to the next function in the value stream, the lead time for that process block is 7.5 hours. Of that time, 30 minutes is process time. In other words, lead time includes queue time and delays plus process time. Figure 3.4 illustrates the relationship between process time and lead time. Note: In value streams with defined service level agreements (SLAs) between two departments, be careful to document the *actual* lead time, not the lead time stated in the agreement.

FIGURE 3.4 Process time versus lead time across the value stream

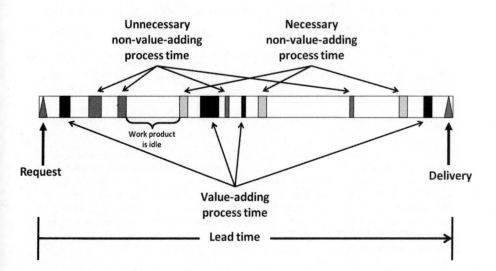

When selecting the units of measure you'll use for lead time, make sure that you take into account the number of scheduled work hours in a day. For example, in settings with traditional 8-hour workdays, a 4-hour lead time is equal to half a day. A lead time of two days is 16 hours. And so on. The same consideration applies to converting weeks and days. A two-week lead time is equal to 10 days in a Monday-through-Friday workweek setting. For longer times that are reported in months, you'll need to consider the number of business days worked per month. In many environments, 22 business days equals one month. Make sure people reading your maps understand the concept of business hours and business days. For 24-hour operations such as hospitals, manufacturing, call centers, and so on, you may be able to safely use clock hours and calendar days and not have to worry about "business time."

Percent Complete and Accurate (%C&A)

As we mentioned in the Introduction, percent complete and accurate (%C&A) is the most transformational metric we've encountered.* It reflects the quality of each process's output. The %C&A is obtained by asking downstream customers what percentage of the time they receive work that's "usable as is," meaning that they can do their work without having to correct the information that was provided, add missing information that should have been supplied, or clarify information that should have and could have been clearer.

If a department reports that people have to correct, add missing information, or clarify incoming work 30 percent of the time

---

*The metric %C&A was introduced by Beau Keyte and Drew Locher in *The Complete Lean Enterprise* (Productivity Press, 2004). Similar to first pass yield in manufacturing, %C&A was coined by the authors to reflect the percentage of information-based work received that has errors and, therefore, requires rework to correct the information or add missing information that should have been received. In our book *The Kaizen Event Planner* (Productivity Press, 2007), we broadened Keyte and Locher's definition to reflect our experience that unnecessary clarification is a third form of rework in office and service environments, and often the most prevalent of the three types.

before they can do their work, the upstream supplier of that work is delivering 70 percent quality. The 70 percent metric is placed on the Post-it for the process that produced the output, not the receiving department. Reporting the %C&A on the Post-it for the supplying process helps ensure that countermeasures address the root cause for poor quality rather than applying a Band-Aid solution at the downstream process.

Occasionally, a department or work team may generate output with a low %C&A that is not detected by the subsequent customer but becomes apparent to customers further downstream. In this case, the team notes each observed %C&A—along with an indication of which process block detected the quality issue—on the Post-it for the step producing the output. You'll see an example of this later in the chapter.

Assessing the %C&A for each process's output is a most enlightening step and can sometimes make the people doing the work uncomfortable when they learn that their output has not been meeting their customers' needs. But with proper facilitation, a blame-free environment, and a mindset that's geared to what can be done to make work flow better, these discoveries can be positive. They provide the trigger for important dialogue between internal customers and suppliers regarding expectations and requirements that, as we noted in Chapter 1, is a culture-shifting benefit of value stream mapping.

Barriers to Flow

While the mapping team is interviewing the people who do the work and/or reviewing performance reports to obtain the time and quality metrics, they need to also discover any additional barriers to flow that are significant and aren't already reflected in the time and quality metrics. Barriers to flow are any actions or conditions that inhibits the uninterrupted progression of work. Excessive lead times due to the presence of waste are not in themselves barriers to flow—

they are merely symptoms indicating that there are "flow stoppers" or barriers to flow. For example, you don't need to note an additional barrier to flow for excessive lead times due to unneeded handoffs—these barriers are visually apparent on the map. Similar thinking applies to rework. While it's an obvious barrier to flow, because it's a natural by-product of low %C&A, it doesn't need to be spelled out.

On the other hand, the following barriers to flow are fairly common, often create significant flow issues, and aren't obvious from the process time, lead time, and %C&A metrics.

Batching
Work is often batched in office and service environments, even when those doing the work don't recognize it as such. There are two primary types of batches: (1) batch *size*—holding work until a specific number of items have accumulated (e.g., entering orders once 10 have been received), and (2) batch *frequency*—performing an activity at a specific time of day, week, or month (e.g., nightly system downloads). While batching always presents a barrier to flow, not all batching is "bad" as is often believed by those new to Lean operations design. To accelerate flow, the reasons for batching must be determined and eliminated whenever possible—as long as eliminating or reducing batches makes sound business sense.

System Downtime or Suboptimal Performance
In some environments, excessive system downtime and/or slow responsiveness present a significant barrier to flow and should be noted.

Shared Resources or Inaccessible Staff
If those responsible for performing the work have multiple obligations and priorities that make them unavailable to do the work as soon as it arrives, this may present a significant barrier to flow. If

staff is unavailable or inaccessible for other reasons (e.g., significant travel, medical leave), this, too, should be noted. When relevant, it's helpful to show the percentage of time staff is typically available to perform the process when the work arrives.

Switch-Tasking / Interruptions

In office and service, switch-tasking and coping with chronic interruptions reveals potential barriers to flow, similar to setup and change-over in manufacturing environments. The mapping team should note this problem if they observe it or learn about it through interviewing the staff during the second value stream walk and it's significant.

Prioritization Rules

During the value stream walk, it's helpful to ask how people prioritize their work to discover differing and/or conflicting rules that may exist, either formally or informally. For example, sales may place the highest priority on orders from strategic accounts, order entry may place the highest priority on a specific type of order, and service may place the highest priority on processing orders for a specific geographic area.

The team's investigative skills will come into play here. Remember, the goal is to understand what is causing delays in the progression of work. But stay balanced and beware: don't let the team succumb to analysis paralysis. The key is to identify only those significant issues that affect performance and flow for each process in the value stream and, once identified, record them on the appropriate process block.

Additional Information

There's a wide range of potential information that may be relevant for gaining a deep understanding about how a value stream currently performs. We've listed a number of these data elements below that often prove important. But, don't let value stream mapping become an exercise in data collection. The team's focus should be on identifying and recording the significant few factors that negatively affect value stream performance. Some of the more common data points that can provide meaningful insights include:

Work-in-Process (WIP)

Work-in-process is the accumulation of work between or within processes. It's a symptom of overproduction, overburden, batching, poor incoming quality requiring rework, variation in prioritization rules, variation in skill proficiency, and so on. As shown in Figure 3.5, work can accumulate in three places, and you must include the quantities in all three places to get the accurate work-in-process quantity for the process you're reviewing: (1) work that's in queue but hasn't been started yet, (2) work that's being processed but hasn't been completed, (3) work that's been completed but hasn't been passed on to the next process in the value stream. To gain greater insights into the current state, the team should also make note of the oldest item in the queue.

FIGURE 3.5 Three places work can accumulate

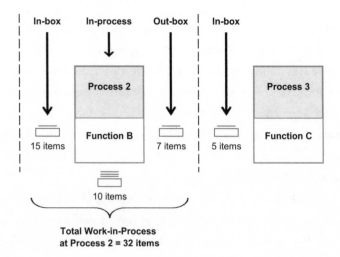

Number of People

We often include the number of people who currently perform the work described on the Post-it. This data is especially helpful if, during future state design, the team sees the need for work balancing or designating resources to a specific value stream. The number of staff can also point to two other potential problems. If staffing is too low to accommodate the volume of incoming work, work will stop flowing. On the other hand, if the staff performing work is very large, it's a good bet that there's high variation in how the work is currently being done and that adopting standard work down the road will require greater planning and follow-up.

In some cases, it's relevant to include not only how many people regularly do the work, but how many are trained and capable of doing the work. You may also want to record the number of people if there is insufficient backup to cover vacations, staff vacancies, and so on. As you'll see in Figure 3.6, the classic value stream mapping symbol for the number of people is a circle with a curved line under it (which represents an aerial view of a person sitting in a chair). We don't include the number of people who do the work if staffing is already known to not be a significant factor in value stream performance.

Number of Hours Worked

It's important to understand whether the people doing the work are working excessive hours or if work is getting done within an eight-hour day. In shift environments such as healthcare and police work, the team members should note if there are two 12-hour shifts, three 8-hour shifts, or some other schedule. They also need to note the total number of hours the operation is "open for business," which will be needed to reflect the metrics in the proper units of measure, described later in the chapter.

Process Effectiveness

In some environments, it's helpful to know the percentage of upstream work that successfully converts into downstream work. For example, it may be important to know how many estimates or request for proposals (RFPs) convert into customer orders or purchase orders (POs).

Work Volume or Demand Rate at Each Process

This is relevant when you have different volumes hitting various departments. For example, the number of requests entering a value stream may be 500 per month, whereas the credit department may only process 200 of those.

Work Trigger

The mapping team should note how people know to do work. Does work arrive physically, or is it noted in an electronic queue? If electronic, is it pushed to the person, or does the person have to seek it out? Are there visual work management boards in the work area? Is the incoming work triggered by a phone call, conversation in the hallway, a fax, or a customer arriving on-site? Remember that the lead time for a process block begins when the work is *available* to be worked on, not when an employee begins working on it, so identifying the trigger will help the team obtain a more accurate lead time. For example, lead time for an e-mailed work item begins when the e-mail arrives, not when it's read; when a car arrives at a drive-through restaurant, not when it reaches the order window; when a patient walks through the door, not when he or she is greeted by an administrative or clinical person.

Other

The team should note anything else that's relevant *at a macro level*. We often remind teams that, during the current state mapping phase, they wear an investigator's hat. Similar to detectives investigating a murder, a skilled value stream investigator has a sixth sense about which leads to follow. Experience pays off, so the more you facilitate or participate on value stream mapping teams, the more proficient you'll become in turning over the relevant stones that hinder performance and enable mapping teams to design a vastly improved future state.

Map Details

Once the team is back at its base camp, it should add the information it obtained during the second walk to the process blocks on the map. Figure 3.6 illustrates the conventions we use for positioning metrics, barriers to flow, and other information on the Post-its.

FIGURE 3.6 Post-it note after second value stream walk

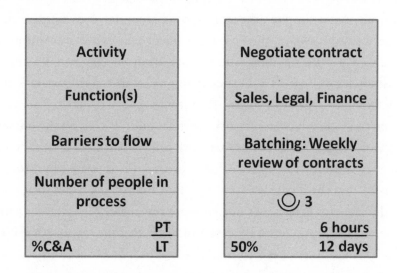

The process time (PT) and lead time (LT) are placed in the lower right corner of the Post-it, with the process time on top. Percent complete and accurate (%C&A) is placed in the lower left corner.

Make sure you include the units of measure for PT and LT, whether minutes, days, weeks, or months. Later you'll need to convert process time and lead time to the same unit of measure, but at this stage you can express both metrics in the unit of measure that's easiest for people to grasp. We typically opt for the unit of measure that yields the smallest whole numbers—e.g., a lead time of 12 business days is far easier to wrap one's mind around than 96 hours or 5,760 minutes. We prefer to express the lead time in one or two units of measure higher than process time to draw attention to the delays (e.g., "Why does it take 2 days to complete 20 minutes of work?").

Finally, the number of employees and significant barriers to flow not already captured are placed on the Post-it in the area between the function performing the work and the metrics.

As we mentioned earlier, if multiple downstream customers report quality issues with incoming work that originated from the same upstream supplier, the team should note each downstream customer's perspective on the Post-it for the process where the output is produced. Figure 3.7 illustrates this situation. In this case, Process 4 passes work to Process 5. During mapping, workers in Process 5 (the function that receives Process 4's output) reported that, 25 percent of the time, they have to rework (correct, add, or clarify) the incoming work from Process 4 before they can perform their own work so, at that point, the %C&A for Process 4 (as reported by Process 5) is 75 percent. Process 7 reported that half of the time, they, too, need to rework Process 4's output—but this rework is different from Process 5's rework. (And Process 5 didn't detect the rework that Process 7 would likely need to do.) The %C&A of Process 4's output, as reported by Process 7, is 50 percent. In this situation, the overall %C&A for Process 4's output is 37.5 percent, which is obtained by multiplying the decimal version of the two %C&As together and multiplying the product by 100 to convert it into a percentage: $(0.75 \times 0.50) \times 100 = 37.5$ percent.

FIGURE 3.7 How to document multiple downstream customers reporting
different %C&As from the same upstream supplier

Accumulated work-in-process (WIP) is placed on the map *to the
left* of the process block it refers to. We typically use an in-box icon
to depict WIP in office-based value streams rather than the classic triangle or tombstone shape, and we only include the WIP icon
where a delay exists. Therefore, if there's no in-box between process
blocks on our value stream maps, it means that there was no WIP at
that process during current state mapping. Beginning teams sometimes prefer including the WIP icon for all process blocks, using a
zero if no WIP exists. As mentioned earlier in the chapter and shown
in Figure 3.5, remember to account for WIP in all three locations.

Assuming work is being pushed through the value stream (versus being pulled, explained earlier in this chapter), all process blocks
should be joined by dashed "push arrows." If work is truly pulled
between two processes, use an appropriate pull icon, such as the withdrawal arrow included in the list of mapping icons in Appendix A.

Figure 3.8 illustrates the information that will now be on your map.

FIGURE 3.8 Value stream map progressive build: process details

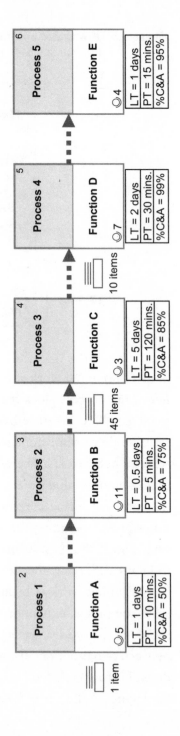

Mapping Information Flow

Understanding how information flows across the value stream is an important part of making substantive changes to the value stream. So it's important to understand the systems and applications that support or inhibit work flow. Specifically, the team needs to identify the systems and applications that each process in the value stream interfaces with, whether these are being used to store and/or transmit data, produce actual work output, or generate management reports—and whether or not the systems communicate with each other.

Value stream mapping is an effective vehicle for visually demonstrating the technology-related disconnects, voids, and redundancies that exist in many value streams. We don't typically include basic applications such as e-mail and Word, but we do include applications such as Excel, ACT!, and Access if they're being used to house data and drive decisions relevant to the value stream.

At this stage, the team should place Post-its containing the names of all of the IT systems and applications in use across the value stream in the space between the customer block and the process blocks (Figure 3.9). The IT systems and process blocks should be connected with arrows, where the head of the arrow indicates the direction of the information flow: an arrowhead pointing to an IT system means that data is entered; an arrowhead pointing to a process block means that data is viewed or retrieved; an arrowhead on both ends means that information is both entered and retrieved for that process.

A lightning bolt–type arrow depicts information that automatically flows from one system to another (e.g., auto-uploads), or from a system to a person (e.g., auto-generated e-mails when an approval is required). Again, the arrowhead direction indicates the direction of information flow. The icon is shown in Appendix A, and examples of it in use appear on the future state sample maps in Appendices B, C, D, and E.

FIGURE 3.9 Value stream map progressive build: information flow

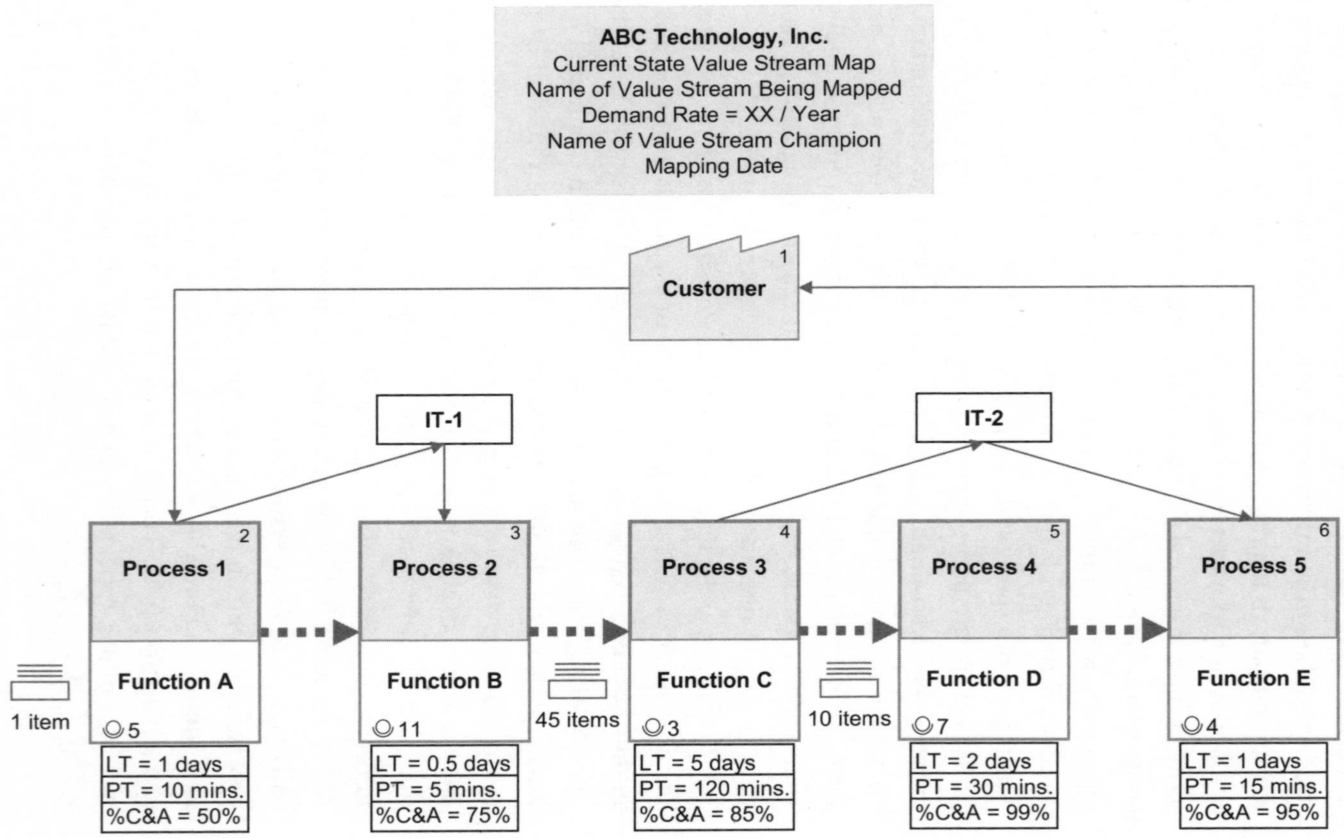

ABC Technology, Inc.
Current State Value Stream Map
Name of Value Stream Being Mapped
Demand Rate = XX / Year
Name of Value Stream Champion
Mapping Date

1 — Customer

2 — Process 1 / Function A
○ 5
LT = 1 days
PT = 10 mins.
%C&A = 50%

1 item

3 — Process 2 / Function B
○ 11
LT = 0.5 days
PT = 5 mins.
%C&A = 75%

IT-1

4 — Process 3 / Function C
○ 3
LT = 5 days
PT = 120 mins.
%C&A = 85%

45 items

5 — Process 4 / Function D
○ 7
LT = 2 days
PT = 30 mins.
%C&A = 99%

10 items

IT-2

6 — Process 5 / Function E
○ 4
LT = 1 days
PT = 15 mins.
%C&A = 95%

This is often an extremely enlightening step in creating a current state value stream map. It's not unusual for a current state value stream in office and service settings to interface with 5 to 15 different IT systems and applications (Figure 3.10). As we've mentioned, seeing the system disconnects and redundancies in a highly visual way is one of the most powerful aspects of value stream mapping in office and service environments. In fact, some of the most significant transformations we've seen can be traced back to leadership's "aha moments" when they've seen the overly complicated nature of their information systems and the overprocessing, errors, and operational chaos caused by the disconnections, gaps, and redundancies. Reflecting the current reality of how IT systems are supporting or not supporting the business in this highly visual way provides the clarity that many organizations lack.

Timeline and Map Summary

The next step in creating a current state value stream map is creating the timeline that demonstrates the degree of flow present, the speed at which your organization delivers goods or services to the customer, and the amount of work effort involved across the value stream.

As shown in Figure 3.11, the timeline falls directly below the Post-its. For ease, you may draw a straight line toward the bottom of the mapping paper. (You don't need to draw the "square wave" type of timeline that the iGrafx software employs.) You'll include the process time and lead time on the timeline. If you haven't already converted to like units of measure for PT and like units of measure for LT, you can do it now as you create the timeline. Remember to note whether your map expresses time in business hours and business days or clock hours and calendar days so everyone will understand, for example, that 24 hours equals *three* business days rather than one day.

86

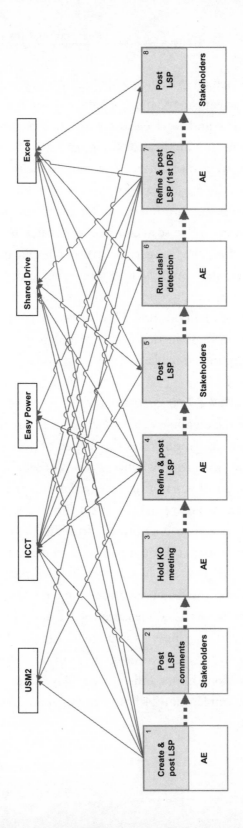

FIGURE 3.10 Complicated information flow

FIGURE 3.11 Value stream map progressive build: summary timeline

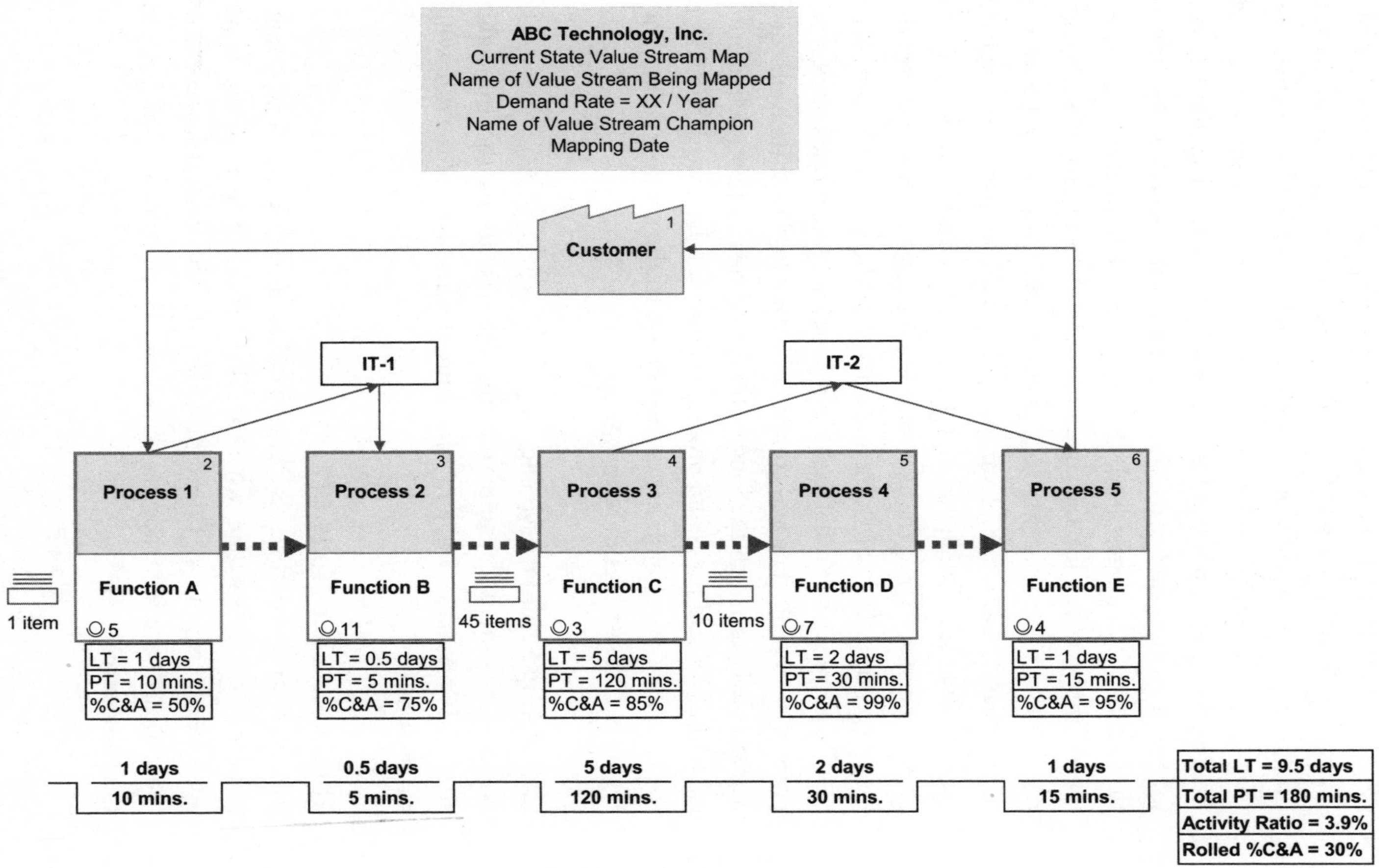

ABC Technology, Inc.
Current State Value Stream Map
Name of Value Stream Being Mapped
Demand Rate = XX / Year
Name of Value Stream Champion
Mapping Date

Customer

IT-1

IT-2

	Process 1	Process 2	Process 3	Process 4	Process 5
	2	3	4	5	6
	Function A	Function B	Function C	Function D	Function E
	○5	○11	○3	○7	○4
	LT = 1 days	LT = 0.5 days	LT = 5 days	LT = 2 days	LT = 1 days
	PT = 10 mins.	PT = 5 mins.	PT = 120 mins.	PT = 30 mins.	PT = 15 mins.
	%C&A = 50%	%C&A = 75%	%C&A = 85%	%C&A = 99%	%C&A = 95%

1 item

45 items

10 items

1 days	0.5 days	5 days	2 days	1 days
10 mins.	5 mins.	120 mins.	30 mins.	15 mins.

Total LT = 9.5 days
Total PT = 180 mins.
Activity Ratio = 3.9%
Rolled %C&A = 30%

87

With parallel processes, the process times and lead times for only one of the Post-its—or series of Post-its—is brought down to the timeline. On maps with only one parallel process block before the work reconverges with the main value stream, you select the lead time and process time from the parallel process Post-it that has the longest lead time and place those values on the timeline. An exception exists if the longest lead time is a "dead-end process." In other words, if the output for a particular process doesn't progress through the value stream, you eliminate it from consideration and take the next longest lead time. Examples of dead-end processes include creating internal management reports and auditing work that has already been delivered to the customer. We refer to the path with the longest lead time as the "timeline critical path."

On maps with parallel paths that have more than one consecutive process block, calculate and compare the total lead time for each path. The parallel path with the longest total lead time is the timeline critical path. The lead times and process times from the process blocks on the timeline critical path are carried down to the summary time line. Figure 3.12 illustrates the convention.

Calculating Summary Metrics

Next, the team will summarize the metrics across the full value stream. We recommend, at a minimum, the first four of the following summary metrics:

Total Lead Time (Total LT)

This value reflects the total time it takes to deliver on a customer request. Remember that, when parallel processes (concurrent work activities) exist, the total lead time includes the longest lead time of the various parallel processes that form the timeline critical path of the value stream.

FIGURE 3.12 Parallel process block treatment on the timeline

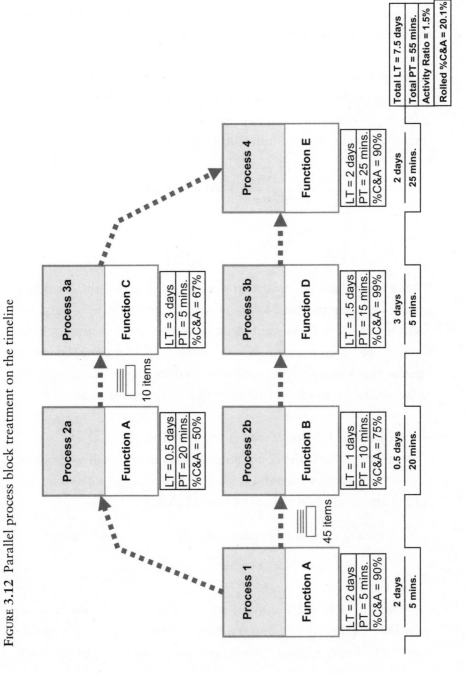

Total Process Time (Total PT)

This value reflects the total work effort required by all functions on the timeline critical path of the value stream.

Activity Ratio (AR)

This value reflects the degree of flow in the value stream. It's calculated by dividing the total process time by the total lead time and then multiplying the result by 100 to convert it to a percentage:

$$\frac{\text{Total Process Time}}{\text{Total Lead Time}} \times 100 = \text{Activity Ratio}$$

$$\frac{3 \text{ hours}}{76 \text{ hours}} \times 100 = 3.9\%$$

It's not uncommon to see current state activity ratios in the 2 to 5 percent range, meaning that, while people are generally very busy, the work is idle 95 to 98 percent of the total time it takes work to flow through the value stream. This discovery, while sobering, begins to open people's minds to the significant need for improvement, another technique for reducing resistance to change down the road.

Rolled Percent Complete and Accurate (Rolled %C&A)

This number reflects the compounded effect of the quality of output across the value stream and is calculated as follows (where the subscripts represent the numbered process blocks):

$$(\%C\&A)_1 \times (\%C\&A)_2 \times (\%C\&A)_3 \times (\%C\&A)_4 \times 100 = \text{Rolled } \%C\&A$$

$$(0.50 \times 0.75 \times 0.85 \times 0.99 \times 0.95) \times 100 = 30.0\%$$

Like Activity Ratio, the current state Rolled %C&A can be quite sobering. It's not all that unusual for the team members responsible for a process to report that they receive input that has to be reworked

100 percent of the time (%C&A = 0). And even when that condition doesn't exist, the Rolled %C&A for many current state value streams in office and service settings is only 1 to 10 percent, meaning that 90 to 99 percent of the work has to be reworked at some point across the value stream. In value streams with parallel paths, the Rolled %C&A includes the %C&A for *all* process blocks on the map.

Total Labor Process Time

This value reflects the collective work effort required by *all* functions involved in the value stream and is used to calculate capacity gains due to reduced process time in the future state design. The total labor process time is the sum of the process times of *all* of the process blocks on the map, including the timeline critical path blocks and all other parallel path process blocks, even if they're part of a dead-end path.

Total Labor Effort

This calculation reflects the total human effort (annualized) that's required to perform the work within the scope of the value stream being mapped. It's calculated by multiplying the total labor process time by the number of times the value stream processes customer requests each year.

Labor effort can be expressed in the total hours needed to operate the value stream (as calculated above), the equivalent number of FTEs (full-time equivalents) needed to operate the value stream, or the labor dollars that the value stream consumes based on a median salary or wage for the value stream workers. The FTE version is calculated as follows:

$$\frac{\text{Total Process Time per Occurrence (in hours)} \times \text{\# Occurrences per Year}}{\text{\# Available Work Hours per Employee per Year}} = \text{\#FTEs}$$

$$\frac{3.0 \text{ Hours per Occurrence} \times 25{,}000 \text{ Occurrences per Year}}{1{,}850 \text{ Available Work Hours per Employee per Year}} = 40.5 \text{ FTEs}$$

A key component in the formula to determine the number of FTEs is the available work hours per year. To determine available work hours, begin with the number of paid hours per year (in organizations that pay their staff for 40 hours per week, it's typically 2,080). From the total paid hours, subtract all *paid* time off, including vacation time, holidays, sick days, and paid breaks. Also subtract the time consumed by other routine events that consume workers' available time (e.g., 30-minute daily meetings). We don't typically include other types of meetings, training sessions, time away from one's work to make copies, and so on. This is a directional measurement; we opt for accuracy over precision.

As you can probably sense, the most important element of this calculation comes into play during future state design when the team finds ways to reduce the labor effort required to operate the value stream. *Freed capacity* is the result of process time reduction through the elimination of wasteful activities and/or optimizing work. For organizations that want to absorb growth without a commensurate increase in labor expense, freeing capacity is an important objective. Chapter 4 will go more deeply into the reasons for and benefits of freeing capacity—and how to use freed capacity in a responsible way.

We recommend that the mapping team prepare a table similar to Table 3.1 on a flipchart or on an extra segment of mapping paper to display the key summary metrics for the current state and, later, the projected metrics for the future state design.

While the summary metrics give tremendous insight into value stream performance, you may want to include additional metrics that reflect the current state of the value stream—time-related (call center hold times), service (percentage of on-time deliveries) financial (percentage repeat sales), people-based (number of sick days or turnover), and so on. The user-defined areas on Table 3.1 serve as a reminder that each value stream has unique performance requirements that will vary depending on the business problems value stream mapping has been employed to help address.

TABLE 3.1 Basic current state value stream performance metrics

Metric	Current State	Projected Future State	Projected % Improvement
Total Lead Time	9.5 days		
Total Process Time	180 minutes		
Activity Ratio	3.9%		
Rolled % Complete & Accurate	30.0%		
User defined			
User defined			

Using Multiple Summary Timelines

An alternate approach to mapping value streams that contain distinct preproduction or preservice segments was first described by authors Beau Keyte and Drew Locher in their book *The Complete Lean Enterprise*. Rather than create a continuous linear map, this method utilizes multiple summary timelines to visually differentiate preservice (or preproduction) activities from the actual delivery of services (or physical production of product) (Figure 3.13). Preservice process blocks often include activities such as entering an order, processing a request, generating a quote, preparing a customer requirements document, scheduling the actual service, and so on.

(continued)

When creating a map with this type of layout, place the customer icon in the upper right portion of the map, and arrange the preservice process blocks from right to left along the top portion of the map. The process blocks that represent the delivery of service or the physical production of producing a good are placed below the preservice/preproduction process blocks and arranged from left to right.

Then, you draw the multiple timelines. To create a map that's easier on the eye, the preservice/preproduction timeline is typically drawn above the preservice process blocks and, like the corresponding process blocks, the flow of this timeline moves from right to left. The summary timeline box generally appears on the left side of the preservice/preproduction timeline.

The second timeline, which reflects the work required to actually deliver the service or produce the good, is handled like the timeline description earlier in this chapter; it's placed below the process blocks and arranged from left to right, with the summary timeline box on the right end of the timeline.

You can then add the values in the two summary timeline boxes to get a summary for the complete value stream, which represents the full customer experience from request to delivery.

In some cases, we've added a third row of process blocks near the bottom of the map and a third timeline that represents the postservice or postproduction activities that are required to transform the delivered services or goods into payment. Integrating these process blocks results in a true "quote-to-cash" value stream map.

FIGURE 3.13 Multiple timelines

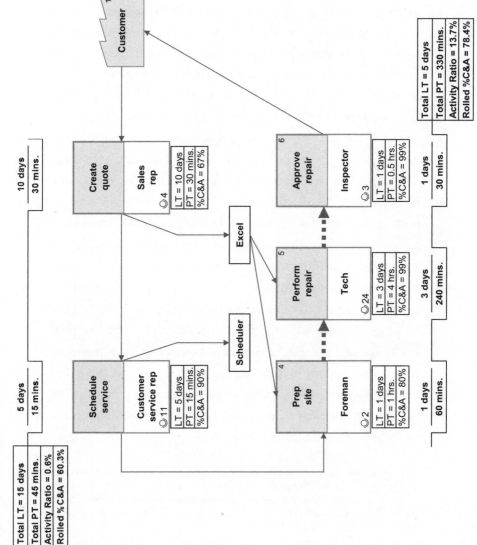

Breaking the map into these multiple segments has many benefits. Visually, this type of layout helps orient the reader to the phases involved in fulfilling a customer request. From a logistics perspective, this layout can often make better use of the "real estate" you have available for a value stream map, whether on a wall or on paper. And finally, from an improvement point of view, maps laid out in this fashion help highlight specific segments where performance is an issue. We had one client where production lead time was reduced from 10 days to 2 days, but preproduction was six weeks. With the two-line map, it became very clear that the improvement focus needed to be on the front-end activities.

The maps in Appendix B illustrate a variation on the multiple-timeline theme in that the value step has "preproduction" steps that are expressly excluded from the map's summary timeline, the reasons for which are explained in the Appendix description. In this case, the team didn't see value in adding a second timeline.

Another way to analyze the time and quality metrics for separate sections of your value stream is to insert vertical lines to visually segment the map. For example, a quote-to-cash value stream map could be segmented into the sales, operations, and billing components for deeper analysis, and the metrics for each section could be analyzed similar to the process described above.*

---

*The iGrafx software we typically use for archiving the maps after they're produced using paper and Post-its doesn't currently allow you to create separate summary blocks for map segments unless you create separate timelines as described above. When using iGrafx, we manually add summary blocks for each segment.

GAINING A DEEP AND COLLECTIVE UNDERSTANDING

In summary, creating the current state value stream map should be viewed as a discovery activity. Similar to a CSI investigator, the mapping team's role is to unearth the truth about the current state design, its performance, and the barriers that prevent flow or otherwise hinder performance. The team may wish to use additional tools to help discover problems and opportunities for improvement, such as spaghetti diagrams that depict the movement of people and material, the flow of information, or communication patterns; staff surveys to assess job satisfaction and engagement levels; pictures and videos of how work gets done; and samples of work output, to name a few. In the latter case, it's sometimes helpful to tape samples of the work output directly on the map. The bottom line: the team shouldn't be limited to the value stream walk to gain the information it needs to gain a deep understanding about the current state.

It's worth repeating that there's as much art in creating value stream maps as science. Remember that value stream maps serve as visual storyboards that not only clarify how work gets done, but also reveal problems. Your current state map should reflect as closely as possible how a customer request is transformed into a good or service and delivered to the customer. Figure 3.14 lists common findings that are revealed through the current state mapping process.

As we mentioned in Chapter 1, we find high value in holding briefings at the end of each phase of the mapping process. The briefings help build support for improvement and alignment across leadership teams. The current state briefing provides the opportunity for a broader group to see what the mapping team now sees, and learn what the mapping team now understands about the value stream as it currently operates. This degree of collective understanding helps reduce resistance to future state design decisions. While the current state briefing is often sobering, it's a helpful psychological space from which to accept the need for change and generate innovative future state thinking, the subject of Chapter 4.

FIGURE 3.14 Common process findings

- Loopbacks
- Unnecessary handoffs
- Rework due to errors and lack of clarity
- Batching
- Functions missing or getting involved too early or too late in the process
- Redundant activities
- High variation in how work is performed
- No documented standard work
- Excessive inspection (review, approval, audits)
- Overspecialization of staff
- Existing technology not fully leveraged
- Underutilization of skills
- Compliance overkill
- Delays due to juggling multiple responsibilities
- Push and overburden

4

Designing the Future State

Once the mapping team has gained a deep understanding about the current state, it's time to begin designing the future state. If team members have had an evening to mull over the current state findings, it's likely that they will begin the future state design day filled with both enthusiasm and trepidation. The clean slate and hope-for-a-better-tomorrow that the future state design phase brings can be invigorating, particularly if the current state is rife with problems and opportunities for improvement. After all, designing the ability to operate with fewer customer complaints, less firefighting, and reduced interdepartmental tension brings tremendous hope to leaders and their staffs who may be feeling the pressure from an underperforming value stream. But a clean slate with few boundaries can be overwhelming, especially to beginning mappers.

Because the future is infinite and there are often multiple ways to achieve the same end, there is no single "right" future state map. In fact, if given the opportunity, two different mapping teams could very well create two different future state maps that both meet the improvement objectives set forth. The knowledge that there isn't a perfect map should give beginning mappers solace, but it may also produce a degree of anxiety as uncertainty often does. This is where a skilled facilitator is worth his or her weight in gold. Once you begin the future state design phase, the tenor of the activity shifts from one of fact-finding and discovery to one of innovation and creativity. Accordingly, the facilitator's role shifts from a coach who helps a team uncover and analyze "what is"—a left-brain activity—to a coach who inspires a team to innovate and design "what could be"—a right-brain activity. Skilled facilitators can easily shift between these two roles.

Future State Design: Overview

As we begin future state design considerations, we are assuming that your organization is delivering services and/or producing goods and services that your customers value. Obviously, it would make no sense to spend valuable time and resources improving a value stream that delivers a product your customers don't want. One of the misunderstandings we encounter when working with clients and improvement professionals is that Lean is all about creating flow. While flow is vitally important in building high-performing value streams, making the "wrong work" flow isn't a wise use of time and resources. From a macro perspective, there are three overall considerations to address when designing the future state: determining the work that should be done, making that work flow, and managing the work to achieve continuously improved performance.

Before we go into the specific steps for designing the future state, let's take a closer look at each of these considerations. We begin with determining the "right work": which processes and steps are required for the value stream to operate optimally?

Determining the "Right Work"

Remember that we define optimal performance as delivering customer value in a way in which the organization incurs no unnecessary expense; the work flows without delays; the organization is 100 percent compliant with all local, state and federal laws; the organization meets all customer-defined requirements; and employees are safe and treated with respect. In other words, the work should be designed to eliminate delays, improve quality, and reduce unnecessary cost, labor effort, and frustration.

In the Lean community, improvement has rightly been focused on adding value through the elimination of waste (muda), unevenness (mura), and overburden (muri). As we mentioned in Chapter 3, there are eight categories of waste: overproduction, overprocessing, errors, inventory, waiting, transportation, motion, and underutilization of people (in terms of experience, knowledge, skills and creativity).

In most value streams, there's plenty of waste to be eliminated. But, it's important to remember that there are two ways to eliminate waste: eliminating work and *adding* work. Adding work is sometimes viewed as a no-no for people who mistake "removing waste" for solely *removing* activities. But, as we'll describe below, if adding an activity upstream creates a net gain for the overall value stream, so be it.

Similarly, given the ultimate goal of optimal performance for the entire value stream, one department may need to take on additional work and/or people, redistribute authority, give up some of its existing work and/or people, give up equipment, or relocate staff. This shift may challenge prevailing mindsets and behaviors around resource allocation, budget creation and management, problem solving, and improvement. Embracing value stream thinking is a mark of an organization that has successfully shifted from siloed thinking (what's best for me and my team?) to holistic thinking (what's best for the customer and the company?). Value stream improvement requires strong team-player mindsets and mapping team members who are comfortable designing for the greater good.

Removing Processes and Process Steps

When you remove work effort from a value stream—assuming that the removal doesn't create a need for new work that takes even more effort to accomplish—you remove operational cost. We find that discussing which processes can be eliminated is often one of the easier discussion points during future state design. The facilitator should remind less experienced teams that they shouldn't remove work for the sake of removing work. Activities should be removed when it is determined that they are truly unnecessary.

As we mentioned in Chapter 3, all work effort is classified as value-adding, necessary non-value-adding, or unnecessary non-value-adding. In terms of priorities, mapping teams should place their greatest attention on removing unnecessary non-value-adding activities, followed by reducing the work effort to perform necessary non-value-adding work (and finding ways to convert work that appears to be necessary non-value-adding to unnecessary non-value-adding), and lastly on reducing the work effort to perform value-adding activities. In rare cases, teams can accomplish all three objectives, but if you have to make a choice due to time constraints, this is the prioritization order we recommend.

Removing work effort may require the team to eliminate not merely the work activities, but also the *need* for that effort. For example, if it seeks to remove an inspection step that has existed to "ensure" quality, the future state design also needs to include quality-at-the-source improvements that eliminate the need for the inspection process. If the team seeks to reduce batching, it needs to remove whatever staffing, systems, equipment, physical environment, or mindset constraints created the need for batching in the first place.

In most heavily siloed office and service environments, the steepest lead time reductions are often achieved by reducing handoffs. To achieve this type of streamlined flow, you may need to cross-train staff and create robust process management systems to assure that unnecessary handoffs don't creep back into the value stream.

IT systems, applications, and the transactions that feed them also offer an opportunity to reduce work effort. During the current state discovery phase, it's not uncommon to learn that a work team enters data into an Excel spreadsheet, a database, or an application that is a legacy process and no longer needed. Or the activity may be needed, but can be accommodated more effectively and efficiently by using an existing application or system that has greater capabilities or is more integrated within the family of IT systems that the organization already relies upon. Consistent with the adage "creativity before capital," our mapping teams often discover the untapped potential not only of human beings but also of existing IT applications and systems.

A common behavior is to feel compelled to start improving the value stream at the micro level and focus on reducing process time. However, an interesting phenomenon occurs when teams maintain a macro perspective: process time reductions become a by-product of addressing the IT systems and barriers to flow at a macro level. The facilitator may frequently need to redirect the team to help them stay focused on the macro and eliminate the easy-to-see waste within the value stream. Going into the weeds (process-level analysis) comes later as you execute the transformation plan and define and document standard work via smaller PDSA cycles.

It's important to remember that reducing process time will free capacity (people). If freeing capacity results in a decision to lay off people, there will be unintended negative consequences. Companies that have the greatest success with sustained Lean transformation make an up-front commitment that eliminating work won't result in eliminating people. It's the work that's non-value-adding, not the people. As described in a sidebar later in this chapter, there are a variety of significant ways that organizations can leverage capacity that is freed up as a result of eliminating work. If you use freed capacity to lay off staff, it's a sign of disrespect. You can be assured that employee interest in further improvement activities will plummet and you will be unable to experience successful value stream improvement efforts in the future. Remember that in office and service environments, labor expense is often 80 percent or more of the overall budget. To increase profit, organizations in labor-intensive environments must find ways to absorb additional work and/or bring in additional revenue without hiring a commensurate number of staff, growing the ratio of revenue to expenses as time goes on. Freeing capacity by reducing process time should nearly always be one of the goals in improving a value stream—whether it's explicitly stated or not. But it bears repeating, process time reductions are often a natural by-product of addressing other issues such as poor %C&A or redundant processes and systems.

In those rare circumstances where layoffs are the only way for a business to survive (e.g., extreme market conditions), the organization should perform the reduction in force *before* embarking on a transformation journey that relies on creating a safe environment for the workforce to make innovative decisions. If market conditions deteriorate after the Lean journey has commenced and labor reductions are unavoidable, be sure to clearly connect (and communicate) that the changes are not due to process improvements but rather to market factors. It's difficult to experience high levels of success if people fear losing a paycheck due to continuous improvement.

Adding Processes and Process Steps

To achieve the defined target condition, provide greater value to customers, and build a robust value stream, a mapping team may need to *add* processes or process steps. Where an inexperienced person may assume that adding activities equates to adding labor effort (cost) and lead time to the value stream, the opposite is sometimes true. Consider, for example, the labor effort that goes into collecting payment from errant customers that might have been saved if the value stream included efficient new customer credit checks or some other screening process.

Remember: if the *overall* process time and lead time are reduced and the customer experience has improved, the value stream design phase has been successful—even if the time and effort required within a particular department increases. This is a point that your facilitator should be driving throughout the value stream mapping process, as it's contrary to how many companies think and behave. Until holistic thinking begins to replace siloed thinking, improving a value stream will prove more challenging.*

Another example of the need to add work tasks occurs when a mapping team decides that—*for a limited period of time*—an inspection needs to be added to the value stream to prevent errors from reaching customers. Inspection is clearly non-value-adding: customers expect you to produce high quality goods and services the first time. But some inspection can be necessary non-value-adding until quality-at-the-source is firmly established and the process is stabilized. When addressing quality problems, the team should focus on eliminating the *need* for inspection rather than the inspection itself.

In considering whether to add new processes to a value stream, be careful that you don't add more work to a bottleneck process.

---

*Organizations that make the greatest progress with transformation do so not merely by helping people think differently. It's behavior that produces results, and most human beings behave as we're measured. Therefore, many long-standing organizational practices will have to change to instill holistic thinking—and, by extension, behavior—into the organization's DNA. The way budgets are structured, expenses are tracked, performance reviews are conducted, and bonuses are granted are all examples of paradigms and processes that need to shift. Lean management goes far beyond operations design and applying specific tools.

You want to solve problems, not exacerbate them. Adding processes to a value stream may require companion upstream or downstream improvements in order to improve overall performance.

Defining the "right work" requires open minds and a team's willingness to shift the paradigms under which they have been operating. A key Lean maxim that should guide your mapping team's every step is "maximum results through minimum effort." The team should be bold in its thinking and keep only those processes that are truly value-adding or absolutely necessary for the business to function. All else is waste.

Making Work Flow

The second consideration is how to make the "right work" flow across the value stream without delays and unnecessary effort and expense. Remember the goal: to deliver high quality as quickly and inexpensively as possible. This is where the baseline value stream performance metrics the team established during the current state discovery phase come into play. The goal is to "move the numbers" as aggressively as organizational maturity and the transformation time frame will allow.

For many value streams, merely defining the "right work" will enhance flow and move the needle toward your measurable target condition(s). But the greatest movement will result from intentionally focusing on creating flow. Ideally, the "work item" passing through the value stream never stops. It moves effortlessly from person to person, work team to work team, department to department, division to division with no hang-ups, hiccups, headaches, or delays. So at this point, the team members should ask themselves a key question: What is preventing the lead time from being the same as the process time for each and every process block? In other words, what are the barriers to flow as they appear on the surface? What are the deeper root causes for them?

For example, current state batching may present a barrier to flow, such as weekly data transfers, daily testing, handoffs every four hours, delivery twice a week, annual performance reviews, and so forth. But before an improvement team can eliminate batching or reduce batch sizes, it needs to understand and eliminate the *reason(s)* (root causes) for the batching. The reason(s) may be macro enough to be obvious during value stream mapping so that eliminating the root cause(s) can be designed into the future state. Or the reasons may be more micro than value stream mapping will reveal. In this case, the mapping team can note the need to explore how to reduce batching or batch sizes and leave it to the follow-on improvement teams to determine root causes and identify how to address the batching.

Ideally, the team designs a future state that results in lower lead time (LT), lower process time (PT), and higher percent complete and accurate (%C&A) for every process block. But that may not be realistic. In any case, the total process time, total lead time, and rolled %C&A for the entire value stream should be significantly improved. In most cases, the lead time reductions will be greater than the process time reductions. The Lean movement typically views lead time as the primary metric to improve, since focusing on lead time reductions forces problems to the surface. While we believe that as well, we believe that process time reductions are a close second—especially in office, service, and knowledge work settings. However, as we discussed earlier in this chapter, it's critical that an organization approach the freed capacity that is realized through process time reductions in a way that enables growth rather than viewing it as a labor reduction exercise that leads to layoffs.

There are many ways to achieve flow of the "right work." One way is to apply classic Lean countermeasures and improvement tools, several of which are discussed later in this chapter. Other ways include shifting previously consecutive processes to parallel activities, combining tasks to reduce handoffs (which may require cross-training, resequencing, or repatterning work so that downstream recipients can do more effective work), resequencing work (starting work earlier in the process or delaying the start of work), and creating service-level agreements between internal suppliers and customers, to name a few.

What to Do with Freed Capacity

Freeing capacity is a vital way for labor-intensive organizations to increase the proportion of revenue to labor. The effort, though, should not result in layoffs. Rather, freeing capacity enables an organization to accomplish one or more of the following outcomes:

- Absorb additional work without increasing staff
- Reduce paid overtime
- Reduce temporary or contract staffing
- In-source work that's currently outsourced
- Create better work/life balance by reducing hours worked
- Slow down and think
- Slow down and perform higher-quality work with less stress and higher safety
- Innovate; create new revenue streams
- Conduct continuous improvement activities
- Get to know your customers better (What do they *really* value?)
- Build stronger supplier relationships
- Coach staff to improve their critical thinking and problem-solving skills

- Mentor staff to create career growth opportunities
- Provide cross-training to create greater organizational flexibility and enhance job satisfaction
- Do the things you haven't been able to get to; get caught up
- Build stronger interdepartmental and interdivisional relationships to improve collaboration
- Reduce payroll through natural attrition

Managing the Work

The third consideration that should drive future state design centers on stabilizing and sustaining improvements, and embedding continuous improvement into the value stream. At some point during the future state design phase, the team needs to consider two critical questions: (1) how will you determine if the value stream is performing as you intended? and (2) who will monitor and manage value stream performance? Many organizations fail with transformation because they don't put robust systems and measures in place that address these two key requirements for continuously improving performance.

Every value stream needs two to five key performance indicators (KPIs) that are tracked on a regular basis. KPIs are the *critical few* measures that reflect value stream performance, and are tailored to the value stream and the specific target conditions desired. Common indicators include measurements for quality, cost, delivery (speed and customer service), safety, and morale. Additional KPIs that reflect unique financial, customer, supplier, workforce, and compliance-related issues are also common. The key value stream performance metrics you've been introduced to in this book can serve as KPIs, but most value streams benefit from additional measures, such as the percentage of quotes that convert to sales, the percentage of employment offers that are accepted, the percentage of on-time deliveries, and so on. You need to choose wisely: what are the two to five metrics that provide the best reflection of overall value stream performance?

We have found that many processes within the value stream need their own set of two to five KPIs to track performance at a micro level. If each process performs as it's designed to perform, the value stream should also perform as it's designed to perform. The problem is that most organizations have established neither value stream KPIs (remember that most don't even have their value streams defined, let alone mapped and actively improved) nor process-level KPIs. *This is a primary reason why organizations continue to fight fires, don't capture greater market share, don't generate as much profit as they could, have burned-out workforces, and create self-inflicted chaos that they could otherwise avoid.* If there are no metrics in place, how can you know how well the value stream is performing, let alone if it is getting better or worse?

Establishing KPIs that are actively managed is a fundamental requirement for achieving operational excellence. The key phrase is "actively managed." It's one thing to establish KPIs; it's another to use them to drive decisions and improvement on an ongoing basis.

During the mapping activity, the team should determine which KPIs it will use to monitor and manage the value stream, as well as *who* will do this work. Oversight for value stream performance needs to rest with one person—a value stream manager—not multiple functional leaders as many value streams are currently managed. We address the roles and responsibilities for the value stream manager in Chapter 6.

FUTURE STATE DESIGN KICKOFF

We've found that, especially with teams new to value stream mapping, the future state phase works best when it follows a fairly structured sequence of activities—with a little "wild west" innovation (uncontrolled and unreasonable "what-if's") thrown in to get the team's creative juices flowing, break paradigms, and provide the means for achieving a deliberate but aggressive approach to improvement.

Review the Charter

To keep the team focused on the mission at hand, we begin the future state design phase by reviewing the charter once again to remind the team members of the target condition they are aiming to create. We also revisit the scope that was defined for the mapping activity so that the team begins designing the future state with that scope in mind.

As addressed in Chapter 2, there are a variety of benefits to working within a narrow scope. One of those benefits is that a narrow scope helps mapping teams arrive at an initial future state design more quickly. It's easier for the team to stay focused and innovate when it designs to a defined set of conditions. As we mentioned in the scoping section, and as you'll see again later in this chapter, once the future state design begins to solidify, most mapping teams see that their proposed countermeasures* apply to a far greater percentage of the value stream than the narrow set of conditions that were defined in the charter. Again, this is a reason why stepping back and looking at work from a macro level can be so helpful. Process mapping teams often get stalled by excessive focus on variation and differences within processes, whereas value stream maps reveal macro-level similarities.

---

*Countermeasures are hypotheses until they are put through a full PDSA improvement cycle and are found to address the defined problem sufficiently.

We often see current state value stream maps that apply to only 15 percent of the incoming work result in future state maps that apply to 90 percent of the work. For example, in the case of a greeting card manufacturer, the current state map for an enterprise-wide activity represented only 10 percent of the SKUs (stock keeping units) it produced, but the future state value stream map, which was designed with the 10 percent SKUs in mind, ended up applying to 80 percent of the SKUs with a few minor differences. Due to significant differences in the process steps (different product families), separate value stream maps were needed to address the other 20 percent of the SKUs.

Similarly, a software development current state map addressed only 25 percent of the incoming work, but the future state map addressed 90 percent of the work. And, in the case of the outpatient imaging value stream map in Appendix B, the current state map applied to CT scans only, but with a few minor tweaks, the future state design also applied to conventional x-rays, MRI and PET scans, and mammography. As we mentioned in Chapter 2, while you're preparing the charter, you might have to counter leaders' objections to defining such a narrow scope for the current state map. But once you get through the future state design process, everyone will see that this is a highly effective approach to accomplishing the mission at hand.

Review the Current State Findings

After reviewing the charter, the team should review its current state findings. If there's been a gap in time between completing the current state documentation and future state design phases (even if only overnight), it's helpful to have someone review the map aloud to the team from beginning to end, highlighting the key disconnects and waste observed as well as the summary metrics. This step ensures that both the target condition and the current condition are fresh in the team members' minds.

It's also helpful for the facilitator to remind the team that the target metrics will not be achieved by making minor adjustments; bold, substantive change is necessary to improve value stream performance to the degree that most organizations need. If the team is new to aggressively redesigning work systems and the culture is laced with concern and trepidation, it's helpful to have the executive sponsor address the team once again to reiterate his or her faith in the team's ability to design a vastly improved future state. This can take place during the briefing at the end of day one.

We also have the team review the design ideas that team members generated while documenting the current state, as well as the ideas that others submitted for consideration before and during the mapping activity.

Introduce Relevant Countermeasures

At this point, if the team is new to value stream mapping and/or using Lean methods to design waste-free work systems, we'll typically review the countermeasures the team can turn to for improving the value stream. We focus on those countermeasures that we feel are most relevant, given the nature of the value stream and the current state findings.

In many cases, simply getting the basics in place across an entire value stream—standardizing the work, building in quality at the source, and installing visual management—can yield significant results, such as lead time reductions of 75 percent or more, labor effort (process time) reductions of 25 percent or more, and quality gains of over 100 percent. You can go further and faster once you have a stable system of processes, and developing this stability is often a lofty-enough goal. And, for many office and service value streams, making these three types of improvements can take months and may be as far as you can go with the first cycle of value stream improvement.

In other cases, we introduce the team to pull systems, batch reduction, level loading, work balancing to takt time, cells and colocation, work segmentation, cross-training, automation, and other work design and management methods. Naturally, when possible, we turn to some of these improvement tools while we're also helping the team build the basics into the value stream. For example, if batching exists, we typically help the team understand the impact of batching and explore ways to reduce batch sizes or eliminate batching completely in the future state. The same goes for pull systems. If two functional areas that work closely together are physically distant from one another, we'll help the team explore moving the teams physically closer. And in some cases, we'll help the team consider cross-functional work cells.

But what we *don't* do—and caution you to avoid as well—is to pursue advanced tools such as creating a work cell before the "noise" is removed from the value stream. If you can accomplish both at once, great. Value streams in environments where processes are already standardized, regularly measured, and continuously improved are typically ready for more advanced design techniques. But we see far too many organizations and consultants move to the more advanced tools that are often met with greater resistance before teams are able to produce predictable, error-free work that doesn't get hung up for days or weeks on end. While putting the basics in place isn't as sexy and creative as some of the more advanced improvements, results and sustainability are the goal. We are quick to sacrifice sexy for results.

In our experience, most office and service value streams have never been studied in a methodical way. So it's unlikely that you'll completely eliminate your most vexing problems with only one cycle of value stream analysis and improvement. No matter how urgently improvement is needed, how skilled the facilitator is, or how well-intentioned the mapping team is, it's unrealistic to expect work systems that have existed for years or even decades to be completely transformed in a matter of months. Any consultant who tells you that it's likely, or even possible, should be shown the door. Change takes time.

CREATING THE FUTURE STATE VALUE STREAM MAP

After the future state kickoff, we have the team hang a fresh sheet of mapping paper that, to send a subtle message, we often cut 30 percent shorter than the length of the current state map. When possible, we raise the current state value stream map so that it's directly above the paper on which the future state map will be created. That way the team can easily compare where it's coming from and where it's heading.

At this point, it's time for the team members to roll up their sleeves, grab some Post-its, and get to it. Because value stream design is highly situational, it's difficult to give specific advice about how best to improve your various value streams. But we can share our experience and provide some general guidelines.

We're often asked whether we always start at the beginning of the map and build to the end. The answer is no. Depending on the current state findings, it may be beneficial to work backward from delivery to customer request. As we mentioned in Chapter 3, one advantage of working backward is that the reverse perspective can sometimes reveal opportunities and problem-solving strategies that taking the usual course may not uncover. Starting at the end, from the delivery step of the value stream, can be particularly helpful when integrating pull systems since, in those systems, the downstream customer signals the upstream supplier. Other times it may be beneficial to begin with the areas where the greatest constraint or organizational pain lies. That said, for office value streams, we facilitate future state design by starting at the beginning about 90 percent of the time.

Design Questions

When the team members have achieved a deep understanding of the current state and they are mapping on consecutive days, designing the future state often occurs organically—as long as people are open to challenging their existing silo-centric paradigms about how and where work should be performed. But for less experienced mapping teams, or for teams being led by a less experienced facilitator, it's often helpful to follow a more structured path. Once the team and facilitator gain experience, you can adopt a more organic future state design approach that needs less structure.

The following set of questions can be used as a starting point for designing the future state. We've categorized them into general questions, followed by more detailed design questions:

General Questions

- What are the business issues (service quality, product quality, speed, capacity, cost, morale, competitive landscape, impending regulations, etc.) we wish to address?
- What does the customer want?
- What measurable target condition(s) are we aiming for?
- Which process blocks add value or are necessary non-value-adding?
- How can we reduce delays between processes?
- How can we improve the quality of incoming work at each process?
- How can we reduce work effort and other expenses across the value stream?
- How can we create a more effective value stream (greater value to customers, better supplier relationships, higher sales conversion rates, better estimates-to-actuals, lower legal and compliance risk, etc.)?
- How will we monitor value stream performance?

Specific Questions

Touch Points

- Are there redundant or unnecessary processes that can be eliminated (e.g., excessive approvals)?
- Are there redundant or unnecessary handoffs that can be eliminated or combined (e.g., work that can be done by a single department)?
- Are there processes or handoffs that need to be added?

Delays

- Is work being processed frequently enough? Can we reduce batch sizes or eliminate batching completely?
- Do we have adequate coverage and available resources to accommodate existing and expected future workloads?
- How can we create more capacity or reduce the load at the bottleneck?

Sequencing and Pacing

- Is the work sequenced and synchronized properly? Are processes being performed too early or too late in the value stream?
- Are key stakeholders being engaged at the proper time?
- Can processes be performed concurrently (in parallel)?
- Would staggered starts improve flow?
- How can we balance the workload to achieve greater flow (via combining or dividing processes)?
- Do we need to consider segmenting the work by work type to achieve greater flow (with rotating but designated resources for defined periods of time)?

Variation Management

- Is there internally produced variation (e.g., end-of-quarter sales incentives)?

- How can we level incoming workload along the value stream to reduce variation and achieve greater flow?
- Can we reduce variation in customer or internal requirements? How can necessary variation be addressed most effectively?
- Are there common prioritization rules in place throughout the value stream?

Technology
- Is redundant or unnecessary technology involved?
- Is the available technology fully utilized?
- Are the systems interconnected to optimize data movement?

Quality
- How can higher-quality input be received by each process in the value stream (to improve the %C&A metric)?
- Is there an opportunity to standardize and error proof work?

Labor Effort
- How can we eliminate unnecessary non-value-adding work?
- How can we reduce the labor effort in necessary non-value-adding work?
- How can we optimize value-adding work?

Value Stream Management
- Do policies need to be changed to enable improved performance?
- Are there organization/departmental/reporting structures that can be changed to reduce conflicting goals or align resources?
- Do existing performance metrics (if any) encourage desired behaviors and discourage dysfunctional behavior?

- What key performance indicators (KPIs) will we use to monitor value stream performance?
- Who will monitor the KPIs? How frequently? Who else will results be communicated to?
- What visual systems can be created to aid in managing and monitoring the value stream?
- Are the key *processes* within the value stream clearly defined with their own KPIs, standardized appropriately, and measured and improved regularly?

As the team considers these questions, the future state map will begin to crystallize. In some cases, the team knows exactly what the future state needs to look like to meet—or, ideally, exceed—the measurable targets established up front and be completed within the execution time frame established during the charter formation process. In this case, it identifies those improvements and moves to the next step rather easily.

In other cases, teams may need to go through a brainstorming activity to generate a full range of countermeasures that could help achieve the future state target condition established during the charter formation process—or a prioritization process to determine which of a series of ideas will get them closest to the target condition within the defined time frame. In either case, we recommend using the brainstorming process of your choice, followed by placement of those numbered ideas on a basic prioritization grid as shown in Figure 4.1. With limited transformation time frames, the team would likely select those improvements that carry the greatest benefit for value stream performance and that can be accomplished most easily (in the upper right portion of the grid). We use this grid as guidance versus gospel. Organizations often have compelling reasons to tackle difficult improvements before some of the less resource-, time-, and effort-intensive ones.

FIGURE 4.1 PACE chart for setting priorities

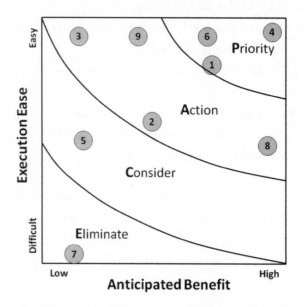

After the team members have selected and prioritized the improvements, it's time for them to document the future state design and estimate how they believe the future state will perform.

Laying Out the Future State Value Stream Map

When building the future state value stream map, the same steps you learned in Chapter 3 apply. If it's relevant—as it often is—the team goes back to the gemba to design the future state or a portion of the future state. Team members write the activities in the verb-plus-noun format on Post-its, and then place the Post-its in the sequence they envision (including parallel processes, if relevant). The facilitator should remind the team members that they shouldn't be concerned about *how* the work will be done. The only thing they should concern themselves with at this stage is the high-level description of *what* will be done. At this stage, the Post-its should only include the process description: no metrics, no department names, and no process block numbers.

Next, the team should decide which functions will perform the work at each process, as well as the projected process time, lead time, and %C&A. In this phase, the metrics are well-grounded estimates by experienced—and now highly knowledgeable—professionals. In our experience, many teams underestimate the positive impact that the changes will have rather than overestimate the results. While it's important to be as realistic as possible, everyone needs to acknowledge that there are a significant number of unknowns at this stage of the transformation process that could alter predictions. As we've mentioned, significant transformation typically requires multiple PDSA cycles; when new discoveries indicate that the team's future state predictions need to be adjusted, so be it.

The team members should then create the timeline and calculate the projected summary metrics, following the same steps they took to create the current state map. They should add the summary metrics to the results table they started during current state mapping, as shown in Table 4-1.*

TABLE **4.1** Basic future state value stream performance metrics

Metric	Current State	Projected Future State	Projected % Improvement
Total Lead Time	9.5 days	3.5 days	63.2%
Total Process Time	180 minutes	160 minutes	11.1%
Activity Ratio	3.9%	9.5%	143.6%
Rolled % Complete & Accurate	30.0%	89.3%	197.7%
User defined			
User defined			

---

*Typically, the total process times and lead times are lower in the future state than the current state due to reductions in work effort and waiting. In rare circumstances, the process time could increase in the future state due to adding important activities that were missing in the current state. While one aims for a higher activity ratio to reflect greater flow, the activity ratio could be lower in the future state due to an increased process time or if the percentage reduction of process time is greater than the percentage reduction of lead time. See Appendix D for an example of this.

The next step is to note the improvements that need to be made to realize the future state that the mapping team has designed. These improvements are visually depicted by using "kaizen bursts," irregularly-shaped icons on a future state map that describe the improvements that need to be executed to realize the future state. (We frequently see kaizen bursts on current state maps, but it's best to place them on the "blueprint map"—the future state you seek to build. Since the future state map is eventually socialized and posted, you want to show what the value stream will look like in the future, together with the changes required to get there. The current state map represents just that: the current state.)

In most cases, the kaizen bursts should describe the improvement generally (what), not specifically (how). Remember, value stream mapping is a strategic leadership activity that is part of a macro PDSA cycle. Designing and making specific improvements requires a series of micro PDSA cycles and heavy involvement from the front lines. You want those closest to the work designing tactical-level improvements rather than leaders who are too far from the work to determine exactly what should be done to reach a target condition. For example, the value stream mapping team could discover that work needs to be standardized. In this case, the kaizen burst should say exactly that: standardize work. The workers involved with actual improvement will determine (with guidance and boundaries) what form the standardized work should take: a checklist to reduce errors, a visual and concise SOP (standard operating procedure), laminated work instructions, etc. Also remember that the kaizen bursts contain hypotheses that need to be put through their PDSA paces before being incorporated into the value stream. As shown in Figure 4.2 (which is the same as Figure 1.4 in Chapter 1), the bursts are placed closest to the process block they refer to.

Future state design requires a fair amount of innovative and critical thinking—thinking that is significantly different from the think-

FIGURE 4.2 Basic future state value stream map

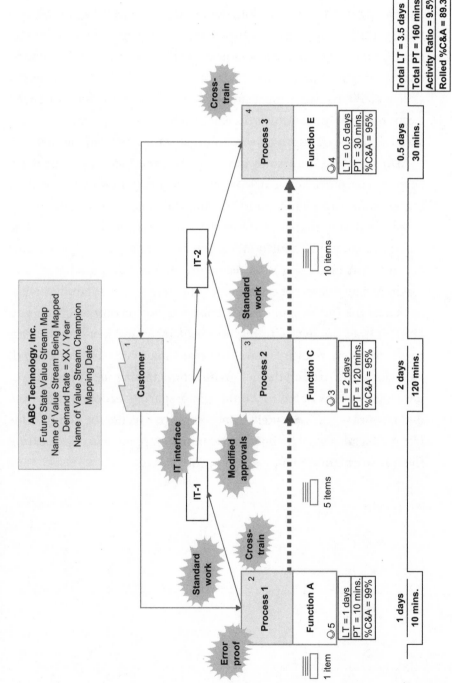

ing required to gain a deep understanding about the current state. Depending on the organization, designing an improved state can also require thick skin, intestinal fortitude, and a hefty dose of courage. Challenging long-standing organizational beliefs, policies, behaviors, and paradigms isn't for the faint of heart. This is, again, where a skilled facilitator is a critical success factor. Otherwise, inexperienced teams may opt for easy over necessary, which won't generate the substantive degree of improvement an organization typically needs.

During the future state design phase, the facilitator's primary role shifts from leading discovery to inspiring innovation, reducing resistance to change, and helping the team gain consensus on a holistic design that best serves the value stream's customers. The facilitator should be skilled in reading body language, helping teams get unstuck, mediating disagreements, challenging paradigms, and teaching new design concepts that the team may not be familiar with.

Once the future state map is complete, we recommend that you hold another briefing with relevant leadership and key stakeholders to uncover any relevant issues the team may not have considered, gain consensus around the design direction and degree of aggressiveness the team has opted for, and begin preparing leaders for the time and resources that will likely be necessary to execute the design. This last goal leads us to the final phase in the mapping activity: creating the transformation plan, the subject of Chapter 5.

5

Developing the Transformation Plan

E xecution. It's the focus of dozens of business books, hundreds of white papers, and thousands of conversations between frustrated executives and their teams. Every author, B-school professor, and consultant seems to have a theory—and often a method—for combating the pesky problem of getting things done. We boil it all down to five unavoidable facts: you need a well-crafted plan, consensus around that plan, the discipline to stick with it, the wisdom to know when to adjust the plan, and the restraint to deviate from the plan only when absolutely necessary. There's a big difference between needing to change a plan because new data or new conditions warrant it and deviating from a plan because an avoidable distraction has taken away the focus of an improvement team.

The third day of a three-day value stream mapping activity centers on creating an executable plan for making the improvements that are needed to realize the future state design. Figure 5.1 illustrates

FIGURE 5.1 Sample Value Stream Transformation Plan

Value Stream Transformation Plan

Value Stream	Outpatient Imaging
Executive Sponsor	Allen Ward
Value Stream Champion	Paul Scanner
Value Stream Mapping Facilitator	Dave Parks
Date Created	10/18/12

Scheduled Review Dates
1-Nov-12
21-Nov-12
13-Dec-12
10-Jan-13

FS VSM Block #	Measurable Target	Proposed Countermeasure	Exec. Method*	Owner	Planned Timeline for Execution (1–12)	Status
2	Improve quality of referral to 85%	Implement standard work for referral process	KE	Sean Michaels	↑ (3)	100%
3,4	Reduce lead time between scheduling and preregistration step to 45 minutes	Cross-train and co-locate work teams	Proj	Dianne Marie	↑ (5–11)	75%
4	Only one check in per patient	Collect copays in Imaging	KE	Ryan Austin	↑ (7–8)	50%
4	Reduce wait time in waiting area by 50%	Balance work / level demand	KE	Dianne Marie	↑ (6–7)	50%
6	Eliminate 6 hour lead time associated with transcription step	Implement voice recognition technology	Proj	Dave Gerald	↑ (5–10)	50%
7	Eliminate redundant data entry	Auto populate between PACS and Meditech	Proj	Dave Gerald	↑ (4–5)	25%
5	Visually managed inventory; no outages or expired items	5S CT supplies area; implement kanban	KE	Michael O'Shea	↑ (6–7)	100%
6	Reduce imaging LT to one hour	Value-stream specific radiologists	Proj	Martha Allen	↑ (6–10)	25%
8	Reduce report delivery LT to 30 minutes	Increase % of physicians receiving electronic delivery	Proj	Martha Allen	↑ (9–10)	0%
7	Reduce LT at image review to 1 day	Visual metrics and indicators	JDI	Dave Gerald	↑ (3)	100%

Agreement

Executive Sponsor	Value Stream Champion	Value Stream Mapping Facilitator
Signature:	Signature:	Signature:
Date:	Date:	Date:

* Execution Method = JDI (Just-do-it), KE (Kaizen Event), or Proj (Project)

the type of Value Stream Transformation Plan we typically use.* If your organization already has a standard project management tool it uses, that may suffice—as long as it includes connectivity to measurable objectives, ownership, timing, the means to formalize progress checks, and it's easy to understand and update.

Like the future state value stream map, the value stream transformation plan is a living document that's regularly updated. It's best if it's physically posted next to the future state value stream map in the work areas being affected by improvement so that entire work teams can follow the progress. When work teams see the plan being systematically executed—and revised as new discoveries are made and new conditions arise—it sends a strong message that the organization is serious about improvement and that value stream improvement is a top priority. Recognizing this behavioral shift and experiencing fewer problems and frustration in their day-to-day work, the workforce will become even more engaged in the improvement process. We also recommend that the Value Stream Transformation Plan be regularly reviewed during leadership meetings to keep transformation activities tied to organizational strategy, and so that leaders can raise concerns, seek clarification about improvement progress, and discuss prioritization and resource needs. It's also helpful to review the plan with the entire value stream mapping team on a regular basis so that team members can see the progress and results of the contributions they made during the mapping activity.

ELEMENTS OF THE TRANSFORMATION PLAN

We recommend that your transformation plan include the following information:

---

*To download this Excel-based transformation plan, visit www.vsmbook.com.

Value Stream Name, Accountable Parties, and Date Created

The charter header includes the name of the value stream; key accountable parties involved with the value stream transformation process, including the executive sponsor, value stream champion (if you have one), and the facilitator for the mapping activity; and the date the transformation plan was created.

Scheduled Review Dates

To ensure that the relevant parties meet on a regular basis and review the progress being made in realizing the future state, we have found it helpful to set the meeting dates and expectations for attendance up front. For transformation plans with aggressive time frames (less than 90 days), we recommend holding status meetings once a week. For plans that will take three months or longer, we recommend you hold status meetings every two to three weeks. We've found that monthly status meetings are not frequent enough for driving execution and making adjustments when needed. See Chapter 6 for our recommendations for the logistics and content of the transformation plan review meetings.

Future State Value Stream Map Block Numbers

List the process block number(s) that an improvement is targeted to affect. Some teams may prefer to number the kaizen bursts and list them here, but we prefer listing the process block numbers so it's easier to correlate the intended shifts in metrics with the portion of the value stream being improved.

Measurable Target

The measurable target is the specific objective related to the corresponding countermeasure. As we mentioned in Chapter 4, each countermeasure is a hypothesis: if a certain improvement is made, the team is hypothesizing that it will have a predicted result. The measurable target describes what the mapping team anticipates the result will be. By comparing the defined target with actual results, the team can determine if its hypothesis was proven and make appropriate adjustments if it wasn't.

When possible, include process-specific target metrics, such as target lead times, output quality, process time, or any of the other metrics you've determined are relevant for the processes in the value stream. If any of the proposed countermeasures will affect overall value stream performance rather than the performance of one or more process blocks, include the metrics for that here as well.

Proposed Countermeasures

This section lists the improvements contained in the kaizen bursts on the future state map. Remember that the kaizen bursts on the future state value stream map list *what* needs to happen improvement-wise, not specifically *how* the improvement will be achieved. The authority for determining how the improvement will be designed and implemented is given to the people who do the work being improved by one of the execution methods described in the next section.

As we mentioned briefly in Chapter 2, we use the term *countermeasure* instead of *solution*, to aid in creating a continuous improvement culture, which begins with how people think and speak. The word "solution" smacks of an over-the-wall, permanent-fix mindset, which discounts the ever-changing world we work and live in. In reality, whenever a modification is made to a process or product there will be unintended consequences. In practice, all ideas need to be viewed merely as hypotheses; testing and evaluation of the test results must precede across-the-board adoption. Furthermore, the moment conditions change and performance begins to shift, processes need to be adjusted. What may have been an appropriate "solution" days or weeks ago may no longer apply. The term countermeasure more accurately reflects the fluidity that's necessary for continuously adjusting the changing conditions and for shifting mindsets and behaviors, both precursors to establishing high-performing continuous improvement cultures. Improvements are temporary countermeasures, not permanent solutions.

Execution Method

Defining the means by which improvements listed on the kaizen bursts will be executed helps leaders and planning teams determine time frames for completion, resources needed, and so on. We typically classify improvements into three categories: just-do-its, kaizen events, and more complex projects.

Just-Do-Its

We refer to those improvements that can be accomplished very quickly (in a day or less), are low risk, and don't require extensive cross-functional involvement or deep analysis as "just-do-its" (JDI). Examples include improvements such as hanging clarifying signage, moving equipment, discontinuing a review and approval process (once consensus is achieved), and other low-complexity improvements. Improvements such as these are simple experiments that go through a mini-PDSA cycle. They are small, low risk, and easy to test—let's see if it works!

Kaizen Events

Some improvements are executed most efficiently and effectively during two- to five-day kaizen events (KE).* In many cases, organizations are able to group two or more closely related kaizen bursts into one kaizen event. Well-executed kaizen events are highly effective ways to spread PDSA thinking across an organization and achieve

---

*Some organizations refer to kaizen events as rapid improvement events (RIEs), kaizen blitzes, or workouts. If you're unfamiliar with kaizen events, you may refer to our book *The Kaizen Event Planner* (Productivity Press, 2007). The book includes an interactive CD with 15 Excel-based planning, execution, and follow-up tools. Visit www.ksmartin.com/TKEP.

rapid results. But they do require significant planning and careful scoping to be successful. Process flow redesign and development and implementation of standard work are common improvements made during office and service kaizen events.

Projects

For those kaizen bursts on the future state value stream map that include complex improvements that cannot be accomplished within the kaizen event framework, we recommend using a more traditional project (PROJ) framework. Examples include situations where extensive data analysis is needed, the improvement is capital intensive or involves technology modifications, or the improvement will impact external customers or suppliers, to name a few. To avoid delays in the transformation process, these projects need to be tightly managed by a skilled project leader. (For some action items, teams may need to first engage in a structured kaizen event–like process we refer to as a rapid planning event [RPE], which enables a cross-functional team to develop a more detailed execution plan. This is a helpful first step for complex and/or broad-reaching improvements.)

A Note on Daily Kaizen

Some readers may wonder where daily kaizen (also known by other names, such as "quick and easy kaizen," "kata," "everyday lean ideas," and "daily continuous improvement") fits into value stream transformation. We view it as a necessary organizational behavior that enables continuous, incremental improvement, but we don't typically include daily kaizen activities on the value stream transformation plan. We focus the plan on the resource-intensive, larger-scale improvements that are needed to realize the future state design and, therefore, need to be tightly managed within defined time frames. Once the future state is realized, you are not "done" by any means. Chapter 6 addresses achieving stability and making ongoing improvements to the value stream.

Owner

This section houses the name of the *one person* who is ultimately accountable for seeing that each countermeasure is properly planned, designed, tested, adjusted if needed, implemented, and stabilized. To achieve the greatest continuity, we recommend that value stream mapping team members serve as line-item owners since they were part of the team that developed both the future state and the transformation plan, and have intimate knowledge about the problem each countermeasure is designed to address. The owner is not necessarily the individual doing all of the work related to that specific countermeasure but is the person responsible for orchestrating its execution, monitoring progress, and providing updates during the transformation plan reviews.

Planned Timeline for Execution

We find that using a simple visual tool to show the planned start and end points for each improvement is a powerful means to gain consensus, clearly communicate expectations and upcoming changes, allocate resources, and track progress. You can use arrows, colored cells, or symbols to depict the planned time frames for execution. The columns can represent 12 weeks in a three-month plan or 12 months in a yearlong plan.

Status

This section is updated regularly—at least following every plan review meeting. Making the progress section of the plan highly visual (as we do with the progress gradient) makes it easier to see progress and delays.

Agreement

This section can be used in those organizations that benefit from formally demonstrating commitment to transformation. Of course, a signature is only that. True commitment is demonstrated by high degrees of leadership involvement in the months following value stream mapping as the transformation plan is being executed and modified as needed.

FINAL BRIEFING

After the transformation plan is created, the team should hold one final briefing to get buy-in from relevant leaders about the path forward. This is the time to have candid discussions about the time and resources that will be necessary to properly execute the plan, confirm that the degree of aggressiveness matches up with the organization's ability to absorb change, address the need to reprioritize work (if relevant), and raise possible obstacles to success. It's one thing to get excited about a future state design. It's an entirely different thing to see in black and white what it's going to take to realize that future state. Beware of leaders that want to negotiate for shorter time frames than the team feels is prudent. Most leaders have been away from the front lines for a long time and have grown out of touch with how long it takes to plan and execute well-thought-out improvements. (This is why leaders need to regularly visit the gemba so they can stay in better touch with real-world issues and see problems firsthand.)

In our experience, the plan is rarely finalized and approved by all relevant leaders during the briefing. Leaders typically want to talk with others before fully committing to the plan. But we recommend that you push hard to have the plan approved within one week. The longer the delay between concluding the mapping activity and starting to make improvements, the higher the risk that the future state will be delayed.

At the end of the third briefing, the value stream mapping activity is officially done. Three deliverables have been produced: the current state map, the future state map, and the transformation plan. The team has worked hard and should be commended. It's an intense but invigorating three days.

Managing the Transformation Plan

In terms of overall transformation plan ownership, we recommend a sole accountable party. This person is often the value stream champion, as he or she is often high enough in the organization to drive change, but also is closer to the people who will execute at a tactical level than an executive sponsor is. The transformation plan owner typically runs the status meetings; helps troubleshoot if obstacles arise; supports those doing the work to realize the future state; and provides periodic updates to the executive sponsor, the senior leadership team, and whoever owns the strategy deployment plan, if one exists.

It bears repeating: in our experience, the plan review meetings are a key success factor in value stream transformation. They reduce the risk of distraction and help form strong organizational habits around execution and accountability. While we recommend that the meetings be led by the value stream champion (or a similar role), it's critical that the executive sponsor remain fully engaged throughout the transformation process by attending as many of the review meetings as possible and monitoring the transformation plan *by going to the gemba* on a regular basis. As issues arise, the executive sponsor may also need to work with his or her peer group to address policies, resources, and political issues that may pose obstacles to execution success. We find a direct link between results and the degree to which the executive sponsor remains visibly engaged. This is the stage of value stream transformation where many organizations falter. As we mentioned earlier, the purpose of creating value stream maps is to make improvements. No execution, no improvement.

In the final chapter, we'll address how to drive execution so that you successfully turn your intentions into results. Chapter 6 is where the rubber meets the road.

6

Achieving and Sustaining Transformation

As you've likely experienced, executing improvement and sustaining the gains is often the toughest part of the improvement process. The reason: executing and sustaining change requires a different set of organizational behaviors than those required for planning. Whereas clarity and ingenuity are required for creating current and future state maps, focus and discipline are essential for successfully executing and sustaining improvement. Unfortunately, we see far too many organizations with beautifully designed future state maps that gather dust.

In many of these cases, the organization set itself up for failure by not laying the proper foundation for success. For example, if value stream improvement isn't properly tied to business needs, organizational goals and priorities, or if leaders who oversee the functions that make up the value stream don't fully support the activity, the resulting maps are at risk of becoming wallpaper.

Also, if the mapping team doesn't include representation from all of the key functions or is made up of people who lack strategic authority, the future state map and transformation plan have to go through a postmapping sales cycle to gain the support of leaders in the areas that will be affected by the proposed changes. This phase often stops improvement dead in its tracks because, to gain leadership support for the future state design and transformation plan, the team members have to retell the story of the three days they spent together discovering, analyzing, and innovating.

Because of the extensive conversations that occur during the three days together, it's difficult for the people who weren't on the team to quickly gain the deep understanding about the current state that led to the future state map. In these circumstances, the team often finds itself having to lobby for the future state design. This additional sales step can be frustrating to the team, time-consuming, and—if the team members don't possess strong sales and influencing skills—ultimately futile. This is the reason we stress that value stream mapping teams *must* include leaders who can influence and authorize change.

Another problem that we see all too frequently is organizations becoming distracted before they've executed a significant portion of the transformation plan. This is why leadership commitment and organizational focus are key success factors. Improving the targeted value stream must be driven by strategic needs and be viewed as a top organizational priority—*by the entire leadership team*—to give it the sense of importance that is needed to commit to the significant effort involved in transformation.

Let's say your organization doesn't suffer from any of the above afflictions. Great! You're on the path to success. But there's still one critical step in the transformation process that will greatly determine the ease with which transformation occurs. And it's an important step that's often overlooked: socializing the maps and transformation plan across the value stream.

SOCIALIZING THE MAPS AND TRANSFORMATION PLAN

Recall that socializing the charter during the planning phase sets the stage for greater understanding and reduced resistance to change as transformation progresses. People need to understand why change is needed and how the change will affect them. After the mapping activity, a second round of socialization becomes even more critical for success. For example, socializing the current state map across the involved departments helps everyone see how work flows through the system and what the barriers to flow are—often for the first time. When people see the truth about the current state—and especially the metrics around the current state—it's far more difficult to reject the future state design. And when an organization gains consensus about the future state design and performance goals, improvement can occur more quickly and with less organizational angst than what occurs when people lack understanding about why specific improvements are being made.

How best to socialize the maps and transformation plan? Avoid succumbing to the temptation that you can simply distribute a digital version of the map and plan and/or physically post it. You need to *talk* about it. Explain it. Let people ask questions. It's not only a necessary step in reducing resistance to change; it's a powerful learning opportunity for the entire organization. Instilling holistic mindsets and behaviors into an organization's DNA takes patience and practice. A lot of it! To accelerate the uptake, you want to expose a critical mass to the methodology and results as rapidly as possible.

One approach to spreading organizational learning we've found effective uses a technique borrowed from medical education: *grand rounds*. These weekly or monthly gatherings offer a venue for clinical staff to learn new ways of approaching a problem. Physicians present the clinical problems and treatment paths for specific patients—in effect, the clinical PDSA cycle—to peers, medical students, residents, and clinical support staff. While the discussions often have a celebratory tone to them (as occurs when the patient is cured), they also include frank discussions about what didn't work well.

We've experienced good success using this model to demonstrate robust problem solving and real-world application of Lean principles, management practices, and specific improvement tools. These gatherings of leaders, managers, and even front-line staff can also be an effective way to instill holistic thinking and reduce resistance to change.* The agenda follows PDSA in a case study format. If your organization is familiar with A3 management (mentioned in Chapter 1), we recommend you have the mapping team present its experience using an A3 approach.

Grand rounds are best suited for organization-wide learning; they don't replace the need for briefings during the mapping activity and transformation plan progress checks with relevant leadership and the workers experiencing the changes. You can opt for multiple grand rounds as a value stream is being improved or, assuming it's a short time frame, wait until the initial round of transformation is complete and the value stream is performing at its new norm.

If you opt for multiple grand rounds, you might hold one session to summarize the activities and findings in the "plan" phase of the macro PDSA cycle (problem, context, current state findings, root cause determination, future state design, transformation plan) and one or two sessions to share the experience in the "do," "study," and "adjust" phases. Again, grand rounds don't replace the need

---

*For organizations with distributed workforces, improvement *grand rounds* can be conducted virtually. However, as with any virtual setting, learning is directly proportional to the degree to which the participants focus on the content and are undistracted by e-mail, texting, and so on.

for interim briefings during the three-phase mapping activity, during which real-time decisions are made and consensus is built.

Regardless of whether you decide to expose your whole organization to your value stream mapping and transformation experience, at the very least you must socialize the future state map and transformation plan to all of the leadership (from supervisors to C-level leaders) who have responsibility for the functional and supporting areas that will be directly or indirectly affected by the improvements. In the spirit of respect for people, and as a means to facilitate plan execution, workers who are part of the process or those who will be affected by the improvements must also be aware of the mapping activity and the plan for transformation.

It bears repeating: sharing the maps and transformation plan needs to be part of a discussion, not communicated merely as an e-mail attachment. Having these conversations reduces resistance and provides you with valuable insights from those who do the work, which will aid in executing the transformation plan.

EXECUTING IMPROVEMENTS

Of course, the primary goal of value stream mapping is an improved value stream. Creating the current state map is merely the means to gain a deeper understanding about how work is currently done, identify problems and opportunities for improvement, and establish a clear baseline from which to make improvement. The future state map is the blueprint for building the improved value stream. It provides a macro view for how work will flow in the future. Just as it's a waste of money to hire an architect to create a blueprint for a new house and then decide not to build the house, value stream mapping is wasted effort unless you actually improve the value stream.

The transformation plan is where the rubber meets the road. It's the plan for taking action, getting results, and realizing the future state design. But, as good as your plan may be, and as important as it is to remain focused so that you can achieve the improved state, be careful that you don't become fixed on your plan to a fault. Remember, each one of the countermeasures is a hypothesis (we think X will resolve Y) that needs to be proven and executed, or disproven and modified or eliminated.

As you begin executing improvements, you may find that you need to adjust the original plan. After all, each improvement creates a new set point, which can create the need to alter subsequent actions. And you may find that some of the improvements you make create unintended consequences—both good and bad—that the mapping team didn't anticipate. Also, the fluidity of business may require you to adjust to changed conditions.

Becoming fixed on your plan—because it is, well, a plan—and ignoring evidence along the way that your plan needs to be adjusted is a gross violation of the scientific method of problem solving. That said, organizations are more often guilty of organizational ADD (attention deficit disorder) and not sticking to a well-designed plan than being overly fixed on a plan that should be adjusted. Outstanding organizations possess the discipline to execute the plan as designed unless—borrowing from law—the "preponderance of the evidence" indicates that modification is needed.

Think of the transformation plan as a GPS device: it provides initial direction, but it also reroutes you if you encounter road construction, make a wrong turn, or decide to take a slightly different route. You can also think of value stream transformation as similar to playing a sport. Successful athletes and teams make real-time adjustments in response to scores, penalties, and other changing conditions.

At the point where you begin to execute the transformation plan, you've entered the "do" cycle of the macro PDSA cycle and the beginning of many nested micro PDSA cycles (Figure 6.1). The micro PDSA cycles enable you to plan (establish hypotheses) for specific improvements, conduct mini-experiments, study the results, and adjust as needed prior to a final rollout. When possible, we recommend that you use pilots (using a defined subset of the whole, such as a specific geographic area, department, customer group, or product) so you can test, evaluate, and refine the improvement before rolling it out to the entire group of stakeholders who could be disrupted by an improvement that needs more refinement. Pilots are experiments, and carefully planned experimentation is the foundation for robust continuous improvement.

Following this scientific process assures that everyone involved in making improvements is thinking critically and breaking old habits of prematurely leaping to solutions or rushing through execution for the sake of meeting a deadline.

FIGURE **6.1** Nested PDSA cycles

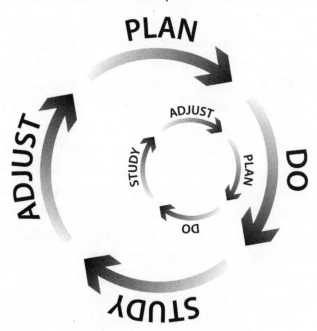

TRANSFORMATION PLAN REVIEWS

As you learned in Chapter 5, your value stream transformation plan should include the dates on which a defined group will review the transformation plan to assess progress and course correct as needed. To avoid distraction, confront real-time obstacles to success, and provide the proper venue for adjusting the plan should it become necessary, it's essential that you hold progress checks on those dates. It's also essential that the team members overseeing transformation have frank discussions about transformation progress, any barriers that exist, and corrective action that needs to be taken. During these progress checks, the transformation plan should be revised if warranted due to changing conditions. If the plan is revised, it needs to be resocialized to maintain alignment across all stakeholders.

As you put the countermeasures in place and see positive results, evaluate if it would be appropriate to start expanding any of the countermeasures to similar processes in different areas or to a broader set of conditions than what the mapping activity addressed. You want to leverage the experience the team gained and spread the organizational learning—and results!—as broadly as possible.

We're often asked who should attend the transformation plan reviews and what the meeting agenda should consist of. In most cases, it's sufficient to have the executive sponsor, value stream champion, and a few of the key owners for the various improvements attend the status meetings. The purpose of the meetings is to assess progress, ensure that all parties are using a robust PDSA approach in making improvement, address obstacles, reprioritize work if needed, and consider new information or conditions that may warrant a shift in the plan.

As with any meeting, we recommend that you prepare a formal agenda in advance and collect relevant background information for discussion to keep the meetings as brief and action-focused as possible. In many situations, it's most effective to hold the transformation plan reviews at the gemba. This provides the team the opportunity to see the real-world results of their work and further demonstrates the organization's commitment to transformation.

The content for these meetings, regardless of location, is situational, but common topics include the following:

Line-Item-Specific Questions

- Which countermeasures have been attempted? What's the progress?
- Did any countermeasures need to be adjusted or eliminated? If so, why, and who participated in that decision?
- Have new countermeasures been identified or adopted? If so, what drove the adoption, who was involved, and what's the status?
- Have any new conditions surfaced that warrant an adjustment in the transformation plan? (Make sure the "new conditions" are legitimate and not merely a habitual lack of focus and shifting priorities.)
- How do the metrics look? Were the measurable target conditions achieved? If not, why not? Can further adjustment be made?
- If the plan has gotten off schedule, what needs to happen to get back on schedule?
- Do the improvements need to be resequenced or start times adjusted?
- Have unintended consequences surfaced? If so, how are they being addressed?

Cultural and Leadership Questions

- Are the line item owners taking (or being given) enough time to focus on the transformation element they're responsible for?

- Are those involved with execution encountering resistance from others? If so, have they been able to address it effectively (through learning and consensus building versus "this is the way it's going to be")?
- Are the resources that are required to put the countermeasures in effect available—e.g., financial, technical, subject matter expertise (SME), and leadership?
- What additional support is needed from the leadership to work through any engagement and resistance issues? (Consider the need to modify policies, reprioritize resources, improve communication within or across silos, and so on.)

Keep in mind that the purpose of these meetings is to assess transformation progress and surface any obstacles that may exist, not fix the problems. If the reviews are managed in this way, these meetings should not require an extensive amount of time. Also, we recommend that you provide regular status updates to the original mapping team members not in attendance and leadership over the areas involved in the transformation and invite them to raise concerns, discuss their observations, and remain engaged in the transformation process.

SUSTAINING IMPROVEMENTS

When we ask leaders and improvement professionals what the most difficult aspect to making change is, they nearly always say, "sustaining." If you're one of those people, we want to challenge your thinking a bit. Sustaining improvements can be surprisingly easy—if you plan well, involve the right people, build consensus, follow PDSA to the letter, and have a strong management system in place. We cannot emphasize this enough: sustaining improvements begins with proper planning, followed by proper execution and management.

Proper planning includes creating and socializing a mapping charter that reflects a well scoped activity with the right team members. During the mapping activity, nearly everything that occurs lays the groundwork for either sustaining or eroding improvements. This includes issues such as how deep the team goes in understanding the current state, how safe team members feel in designing the future state, the degree of consensus across the mapping team, the degree of ownership and accountability for the items on the transformation plan, and the degree of leadership commitment and support.

Once you've successfully realized the iterated future state, you must have two things firmly in place to sustain it: (1) someone formally designated to monitor value stream performance to assess how it's performing, facilitate problem solving when issues arise, and lead ongoing improvement to raise the performance bar, and (2) key performance indicators to tell whether performance is on track or not (value stream management).

In our experience, one of the issues that slows or stalls performance improvement or causes performance erosion is the degree to which there is no one person who's clearly responsible for overseeing value stream performance. If you continue to have many functional leaders watching only their part of the value stream, it'll be very difficult to affect value stream performance in a meaningful way. When everyone's responsible, no one's responsible. You need one person keeping his or her eye on the entire value stream.

The person monitoring performance—often called the value stream manager or value stream champion—is dedicated to, and given the bandwidth for, continuously monitoring and leading improvement across the entire value stream. This person oversees measurement, communicating success, leading ongoing improvement when problems or opportunities arise, retraining when the work changes, and so on. For large value streams, we recommend that this person is director level or above in the organization. Oversight for smaller and support value streams may successfully reside with a manager, as long as the manager has the authority or influence to form cross-functional teams to resolve problems and to make improvements that are closely tied to strategy.

Organizations regularly balk at the suggestion that they need to give one person oversight for a highly cross-functional value stream, to which we say, "Okay, how's your current approach working for you?" Yes, it's a new concept for highly siloed organizations. After all, this would mean having someone manage the value stream who, by virtue of the organization chart, doesn't have the authority over all of the functional areas that make up the value stream. But performing well is the goal, correct? Delivering high value to the customers while maintaining a high level of fiscal stewardship and providing a fulfilling workplace is why most businesses exist. So let's get out of our own way of success and create the means to achieve the organization's most critical goals. You don't necessarily have to rethink your organizational structure (though that may be a highly prudent activity to undertake), but you do need to have *one person* whom everyone recognizes as "owning" value stream performance and who has the authority to affect it.

In mature continuous improvement organizations, value stream managers are sometimes given responsibility for profit and loss across the value stream. In this case, the value stream is often structured as a business unit that has its own core services and that borrows, leases, or purchases shared services from other functional areas across the enterprise. You don't have to go this far, but it's a concept you may want to experiment with. It takes significant organization-wide commitment and necessitates rethinking organizational structure, incentives, implementing Lean accounting principles, and the like.

If your organization isn't ready to structure itself by value streams—on paper and in practice—you can begin with the practice part of it. The value stream champion or manager merely needs to be recognized as the person with the responsibility for value stream performance and the authority to drive problem solving, corrective action, and ongoing improvement to raise the performance bar.

Continuous Improvement

We're often asked how frequently a value stream should be improved. The answer is continuously. We understand that's a tall order for many organizations, but continuous improvement is your only way out of a culture of reactive firefighting, which prevents your organization from excelling on all levels.

While strategy deployment (mentioned in Chapter 1) and value stream mapping are strategic activities, the bulk of ongoing improvement is actually quite tactical. Success comes from having clearly defined key performance indicators for the value stream itself and all of the major processes within it, designated value stream managers and process owners, a strategy and plan for improving the value stream, and a workforce that's skilled, motivated, and authorized to make tactical-level improvements.

We also recommend that you engage in value stream–level improvement activities (the three-day event with leadership) at least once a year for each of your key value streams—and more frequently when possible. After all, if you approach value stream management with the seriousness it warrants, the future state value stream map that a mapping team designed six months ago, and which has been rigorously worked on since, is now the current state. Now it is time for another round of the macro PDSA cycle and a new future state that addresses higher-hanging fruit and raises the performance bar. Another round of improvement will enable you to deliver greater value for lower cost, capture greater market share, keep your competitors at bay, create a healthy return to distribute to shareholders or reinvest in the organization, and help you become an employer of choice.

Value stream mapping is a woefully misunderstood and under-utilized tool for aligning people, visualizing problems, prioritizing improvement activities, and taking performance to the next level. Learning to see and manage work from a value stream perspective is a powerful way to instill new ways of thinking into the DNA of your organization and achieve higher levels of performance. The habits your leadership team gains during value stream mapping activities—going to the gemba; tying improvement to business needs, strategy, and annual goals; true collaboration aligned by a common goal among departments; assessing performance using standard time and quality metrics; and so on—are habits that will propel your organization to greater heights.

It is our hope that this book has provided a solid starting point for you to begin reaping the benefits that come from viewing work holistically and applying consistent metrics—or that it has deepened your understanding and given you new insights on how to take your value stream mapping, and value stream management, to the next level. In any case, as with any learning, practice is the means to mastery. So get going! Practice, practice, practice.

Appendix A
Value Stream Mapping Icons

The icons that are often used in office and service value stream maps are depicted in Figure A.1. Remember that a value stream map is a storyboard designed to visually reflect the current state and an improved future state. In creating maps to reflect work flow within your organization, you may find a need to complement this set of icons with your own standardized icons. Value stream mapping icons should be intuitive and unambiguous representations that enable quick and deep understanding by all parties who will be viewing the maps. Use whatever icons best represent how work and information could or should move through your value streams.

FIGURE A.1 Common value stream mapping icons

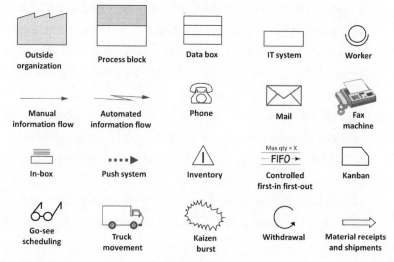

149

Here are brief descriptions of each icon shown:

- *Outside organization.* Outside organizations are external customers, external suppliers, and outside third parties to whom you outsource activities within the value stream.
- *Process block.* The process block houses a concise, high-level description of each process in the value stream in verb-plus-noun format and the name of the function that performs the process.
- *Data box.* The data box contains process-specific information such as process time (PT), lead time (LT), and percent complete and accurate (%C&A). It can also include additional information specific to the process, such as batch size or frequency, percent effectiveness, and other barriers to flow. The data box is placed directly below the corresponding process block.
- *IT system.* The name of each application or system that is used to support the value stream is identified within this icon—one icon per system. IT systems are connected to process blocks or other IT systems with the appropriate information flow icon.
- *Worker.* The worker icon symbolizes an aerial view of a person sitting in a chair and is used to note the number of workers who perform that specific process within the value stream. The icon is typically placed in the lower portion of the process block it represents.
- *Manual information flow.* The straight-arrow icon illustrates the flow of information from people to IT systems, and from IT systems to people. The arrowhead indicates the direction of information flow.
- *Automated information flow.* The "lightning bolt" arrow illustrates the automated flow of information flow between

IT systems, or between IT systems and people. The arrowhead indicates the direction of information flow.

- *Phone, Mail, Fax machine.* These icons are used to specify how information is relayed. The envelope can be used for either electronic or postal mail communication. Other communication icons could include lips or a mouth for verbal communication, a stick figure for walking information to another area, and various symbols for instant messaging, intranet, classified communication systems, and so forth.

- *In-box.* The in-box is used to depict work-in-process, and includes work that is waiting to be worked on, is in the process of being worked on, or has been completed but hasn't been passed to the next process in the value stream. The quantity of work present observed during mapping is written below the icon. Some organizations prefer to use a triangular inventory icon for this purpose, described below.

- *Push system.* The push arrow is used to depict when work is being passed from one process to the next, without regard for whether the downstream process is available or has the capacity to work on it.

- *Inventory.* The inventory icon represents physical items or work-in-process that is queued at each process block. The quantity observed during mapping is written below the icon.

- *FIFO controlled first-in first-out.* A type of pull system where the maximum quantity of work that can queue before a process is established in order to manage overproduction and control throughput times. This maximum quantity is indicated above the FIFO lane icon. When that maximum is reached, the upstream supplying process is signaled to discontinue passing additional work until the work quantity in the queue is less than the maximum quantity allowed.

When the queue becomes full, a temporary reallocation of resources is often needed to assist in relieving the bottleneck.

- *Kanban.* A type of pull system where the downstream process authorizes (via some sort of signal) the upstream process to replenish what has been consumed (e.g., physical inventory, queued work, and so on).

- *Go-see scheduling.* A type of reactive scheduling system characterized by nonstandard human monitoring. As a result of this monitoring, adjustments to work prioritization are made.

- *Truck movement.* A variety of icons, such as trucks, cars, trains, airplanes, ships, and so on, can be used to show how work is physically transported. The frequency of movement is typically noted within or below the icon.

- *Kaizen burst.* These irregularly shaped "starbursts" contain the macro-level improvement activities required to transform the value stream from the current state to the value stream vision. As the improvements are made, the kaizen bursts should be highlighted, crossed off, or removed from the future state map to show the real-time status of the transformation.

- *Withdrawal.* The withdrawal arrow depicts a condition whereby a downstream process pulls material or work from an upstream "supermarket."

- *Material receipts and shipments.* The hollow arrow depicts the movement of physical material, such as raw material, parts, reagents, finished goods, and so forth.

Appendix B
Outpatient Imaging Value Stream

I mproving the outpatient imaging value stream was selected as a demonstration project for a hospital that was just beginning its Lean journey. This value stream was selected for the hospital's first experience with value stream mapping for several reasons: (1) the hospital was facing increased competition from a new neighboring imaging center and had lost market share; (2) the referring physicians had been complaining about excessive turnaround times for receiving reports; and (3) the department had experienced high technologist turnover for the previous two years.

As the charter was being created, it became obvious that the mapping team needed to narrow its scope, so the team decided to focus on its highest volume and highest margin service at the time: CT scans. The mapping activity was held on three consecutive days and included the following team members: vice president, operations; director, imaging; manager, imaging; director, scheduling and preregistration; manager, admissions and patient experience; director, finance; office manager for one of the highest-volume referring physicians; and one radiologist.

The gemba walk was powerful. None of the team members knew how the full value stream operated, and several team members noticed problems in the way the department was physically arranged and the overall appearance of the patient care areas. Discussing value stream performance with the technicians began to shine a light on the issues that contributed to low morale and high turnover. The team also noted other problems such as extended patient wait times, out-of-stock supplies, and delays in report transcription and approvals. On the plus side, the team was impressed with the way the administrative and clinical staff interfaced with patients and the care with which the expensive capital equipment was maintained. Including the voice of one of the key customers on the mapping team proved highly beneficial in defining customer value.

By the end of the first day, the current state value stream map was complete (Figure B.1) and the mapping team was both unified and clear about its future state mission. You'll notice that the Rolled %C&A is the product of the individual %C&As for all process blocks, whereas the Total LT and Total PT are the sums of the individual LTs and PTs for process blocks 5 through 11. The team made this choice because quality at the first process block (referring physician) was a key contributor to poor patient satisfaction and excessive rework by hospital staff, whereas the time in blocks 1 through 4 didn't contribute to poor value stream performance. In this nonurgent outpatient environment, patients often request appointments at a convenient time rather than the first available appointment window. We didn't want to skew the total lead time when the customers (patients) themselves were requesting the delay. The same is true on the future state map.

The future state value stream design phase included a number of "spirited discussions" (as they often do), but once the team members reached consensus on the countermeasures they felt would improve the value stream and created the future state map (Figure B.2), they were eager to begin making improvement. Table B.1 shows the current state and projected future state summary metrics. With the exception of one kaizen burst (implementing voice recognition technology to eliminate the need for a third party to transcribe dictated reports into written form), the future state map was fully realized within five months. The improvements were designed, tested, refined, and implemented through a series of four kaizen events, two projects, and one just-do-it.

One of the biggest aha's as a result of current state mapping was the number of redundant and disconnected IT systems and applications that were supporting the value stream. This revelation led the hospital to shift budget dollars and rearrange capital expenditure priorities to accelerate its conversion to a more comprehensive enterprise solution. Another aha was the degree to which the referring providers were contributing to patient dissatisfaction and delays because 35 percent of the time patients arrived unprepared and/or without a proper physician order. The third largest surprise was the degree to which a cumbersome IT log-on problem caused the radiologists to batch report review and approvals. During one of the follow-on kaizen events to design, test, refine, and implement improvements, the IT team member fixed the years-long log-on problem in a matter of 35 minutes, thrilling the radiologists and cutting a full day from the overall lead time.

This value stream improvement effort led to a stronger partnership between the hospital and its referring providers, resulted in an improved patient experience, reduced frustration for the imaging staff, and improved satisfaction among the referring providers. Due to improved morale, the hospital experienced no technologist turnovers in the 12 months following the completion of the value stream improvement activity.

Improvements in the examination portion of the value stream also created the capacity for the hospital to earn an additional $500,000 in annual revenue without adding equipment or staff. *This is a significant result and one that most organizations fail to fully appreciate.* The freed capacity that was created by shaving *only two minutes* from the time it takes a technologist to conduct a CT scan created the ability for the hospital to perform one additional CT scan per technologist per day. In this five-day-per-week outpatient operation, that gain created the ability for the hospital to earn the additional $500,000. This is an excellent example of how seemingly minor improvements add up.

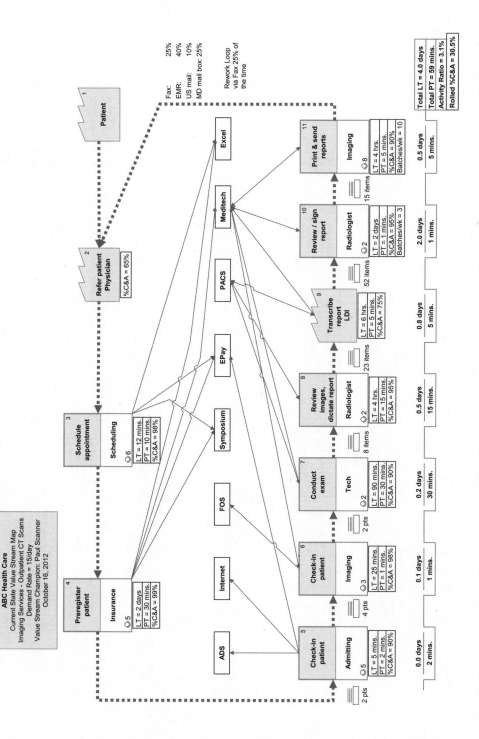

FIGURE B.1 Current state value stream map for outpatient imaging

Figure B.2 Future state value stream map for outpatient imaging

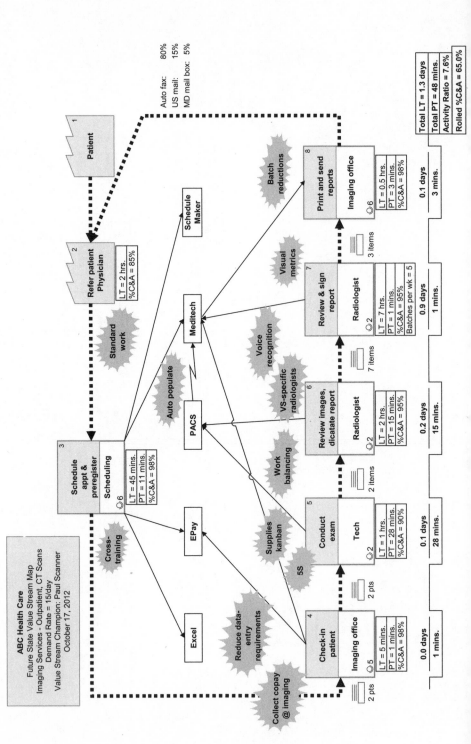

TABLE B.1   Performance metrics for outpatient imaging value stream

Metric	Current State	Projected Future State	Projected % Improvement
Total Lead Time	4.0 days	1.3 days	67.5%
Total Process Time	59 minutes	48 minutes	18.6%
Activity Ratio	3.1%	7.6%	145.2%
Rolled % Complete & Accurate	30.5%	65.0%	113.1%

Appendix C
Purchasing Value Stream

Figures C.1 and C.2 and Table C.1 illustrate the use of value stream mapping to improve a support value stream. In this case, the leadership team with responsibility for engineering design had been receiving many complaints from their staff about how long it was taking to receive the equipment and supplies they needed to design sophisticated electronics for their external customers.

During the initial meeting with the client, value stream mapping was selected over process mapping because it presented a better means for visualizing the significant delays between handoffs and it would help generate alignment among a fractured leadership team. Attempting to map all possible types of purchases didn't seem prudent, so the leadership team opted to map the following conditions: nonrecurring supplies purchases that cost $5,000 or less.

Through rethinking who needed to approve and process the purchase requisitions, eliminating the use of unnecessary software applications, shifting who entered the requisitions into the system, dedicating business unit–specific purchasing agents, and standardizing the work, the team was able to cut the delivery time in half and free managers' time for more meaningful and higher priority tasks, without introducing significant risk into the process.

FIGURE C.1 Current state value stream map for supplies purchasing

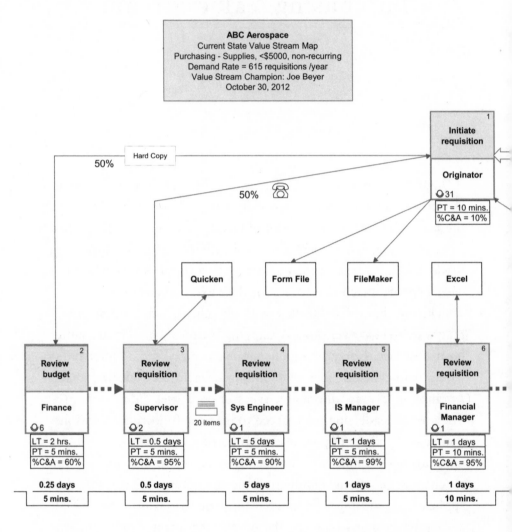

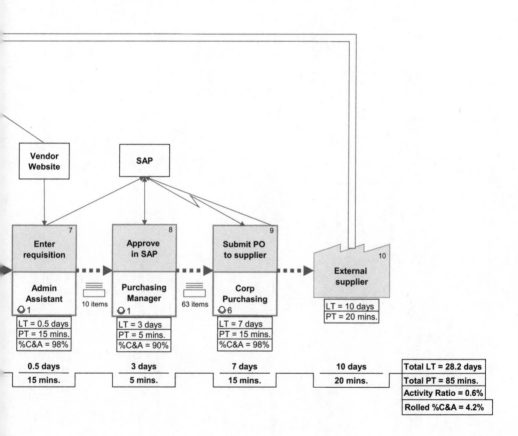

FIGURE C.2 Future state value stream map for supplies purchasing

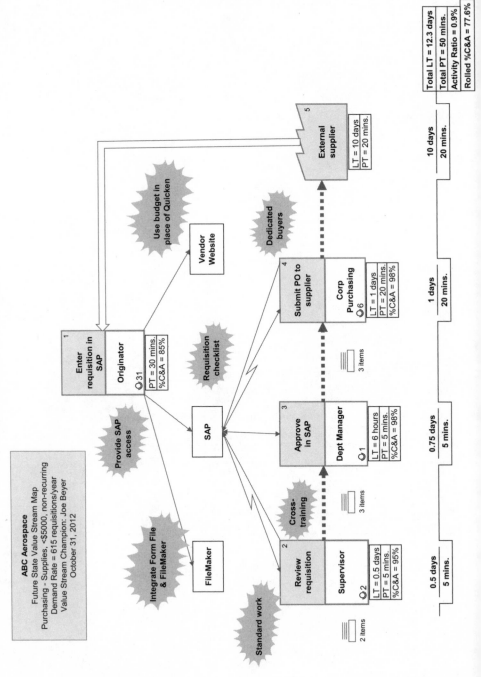

TABLE C.1   Performance metrics for supplies purchasing value stream

Metric	Current State	Projected Future State	Projected % Improvement
Total Lead Time	28.2 days	12.3 days	56.4%
Total Process Time	85 minutes	50 minutes	41.2%
Activity Ratio	0.6%	0.9%	50.0%
Rolled % Complete & Accurate	4.2%	77.6%	1,747.6%

Appendix D
Repair Services Value Stream

The value stream mapping activity shown in Figures D.1 and D.2 and Table D.1 was a kickoff to a company-wide Lean transformation. The company had two customer-facing value streams—repair and installation—and decided to begin with the one that was the higher margin service, was experiencing the greatest growth, and involved the greatest number of employees: repair services.

The improvement efforts around this value stream break from what many would believe is traditional Lean thinking. First, the mapping team decided to centralize dispatch—at least for the short term—to get its arms around dispatching-related problems, leverage technology, standardize the process, and efficiently gain the intel it needed to assess technician skills and design a career track skills development program. Many believe that decentralization represents Lean thinking, but not always. You have to consider the full picture and consider the target condition before making that decision.

The future state map also illustrates a case in which *adding* inventory made sense (compare the frequency of visiting a parts store at process block 7 in the current and future state maps). Many people who are new to Lean automatically assume inventory should always be reduced. But not when it interferes with providing customer value. This client's customer calls are nearly always emergency situations, so taking an additional 90 minutes to pick up a needed part or an additional day for special orders eroded customer trust and risked market share losses.

Notice that the projected activity ratio is *lower* in the future state. This is an example where, because the process time reduction percentage was greater than the lead time reduction percentage, value stream performance appears to have worsened, but it hasn't. Significant improvements are being made to both the process time and lead time, and that's a good thing!

You may wonder why the lead time for process block 2 is 0.0 on the summary timeline. That's because we selected days as the units of measure and opted to only include one decimal point, which rounds to 0.0.

Another element of this value stream transformation activity that's worth noting—and is reflected on Table D.1—is that, at first glance, the lead time reduction for the value stream isn't all that impressive (10 percent). However, notice that the lead time for the final process block (collections) is 60 days on both the current and future state map. The user-defined metric on Table D.1, "total lead time excluding collections" reflects the fact that invoicing is now occurring 7.1 days earlier, which is 63 percent faster than in the current state and creates a significant improvement in cash flow. This is an example of where segmenting the map and looking at the metrics through different perspectives can be helpful.

Realizing this future state took approximately one year, the longest of any future state cycle either of us has been involved with in recent years. But this was a situation where the COO and CEO were both seasoned Lean leaders and had the experience to keep the team on task while they were simultaneously developing the workforce, introducing supporting Lean practices, and developing a continuous improvement culture. If your leadership isn't as seasoned, we recommend shorter value stream improvement cycles.

FIGURE D.1 Current state value stream map for repair services

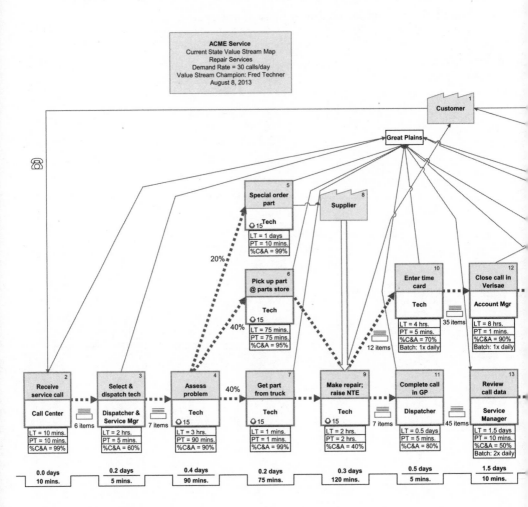

ACME Service
Current State Value Stream Map
Repair Services
Demand Rate = 30 calls/day
Value Stream Champion: Fred Techner
August 8, 2013

Customer 1

Great Plains

Special order part 5
Tech ⊘15
LT = 1 days
PT = 10 mins.
%C&A = 99%

Supplier 8

20%

Pick up part @ parts store 6
Tech ⊘15
LT = 75 mins.
PT = 75 mins.
%C&A = 95%

40%

Enter time card 10
Tech
LT = 4 hrs.
PT = 5 mins.
%C&A = 70%
Batch: 1x daily

35 items

Close call in Verisae 12
Account Mgr
LT = 8 hrs.
PT = 1 mins.
%C&A = 90%
Batch: 1x daily

12 items

Receive service call 2
Call Center
LT = 10 mins.
PT = 10 mins.
%C&A = 99%

6 items

Select & dispatch tech 3
Dispatcher & Service Mgr
LT = 2 hrs.
PT = 5 mins.
%C&A = 60%

7 items

Assess problem 4
Tech ⊘15
LT = 3 hrs.
PT = 90 mins.
%C&A = 90%

40%

Get part from truck 7
Tech ⊘15
LT = 1 mins.
PT = 1 mins.
%C&A = 99%

Make repair; raise NTE 9
Tech ⊘15
LT = 2 hrs.
PT = 2 hrs.
%C&A = 40%

7 items

Complete call in GP 11
Dispatcher
LT = 0.5 days
PT = 5 mins.
%C&A = 80%

45 items

Review call data 13
Service Manager
LT = 1.5 days
PT = 10 mins.
%C&A = 50%
Batch: 2x daily

0.0 days	0.2 days	0.4 days	0.2 days	0.3 days	0.5 days	1.5 days
10 mins.	5 mins.	90 mins.	75 mins.	120 mins.	5 mins.	10 mins.

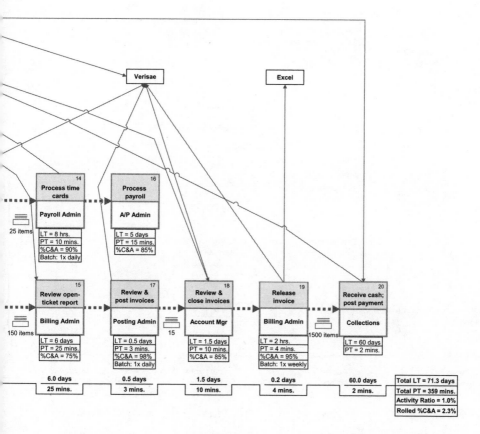

| Verisae | | Excel |

	14 Process time cards	16 Process payroll			
25 items	Payroll Admin	A/P Admin			
	LT = 8 hrs. PT = 10 mins. %C&A = 90% Batch: 1x daily	LT = 5 days PT = 15 mins. %C&A = 85%			

	15 Review open-ticket report	17 Review & post invoices	18 Review & close invoices	19 Release invoice	20 Receive cash; post payment
150 items	Billing Admin	Posting Admin	Account Mgr	Billing Admin	Collections
	LT = 6 days PT = 25 mins. %C&A = 75%	LT = 0.5 days PT = 3 mins. %C&A = 98% Batch: 1x daily	LT = 1.5 days PT = 10 mins. %C&A = 85%	LT = 2 hrs. PT = 4 mins. %C&A = 95% Batch: 1x weekly	LT = 60 days PT = 2 mins.

| 6.0 days 25 mins. | 0.5 days 3 mins. | 1.5 days 10 mins. | 0.2 days 4 mins. | 60.0 days 2 mins. |

| Total LT = 71.3 days |
| Total PT = 359 mins. |
| Activity Ratio = 1.0% |
| Rolled %C&A = 2.3% |

FIGURE D.2 Future state value stream map for repair services

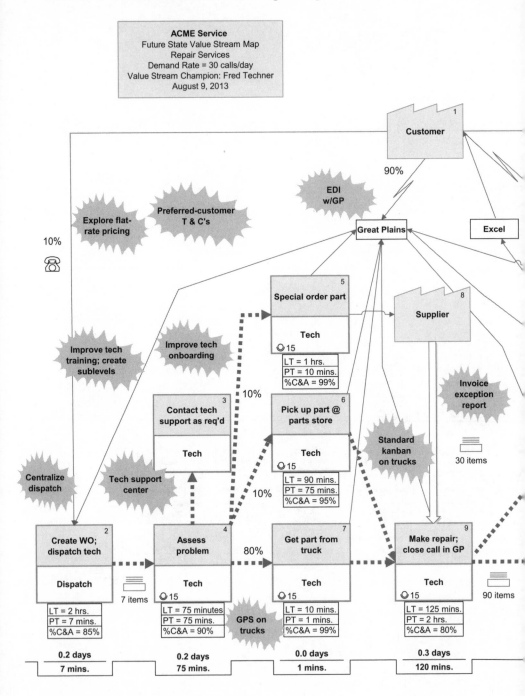

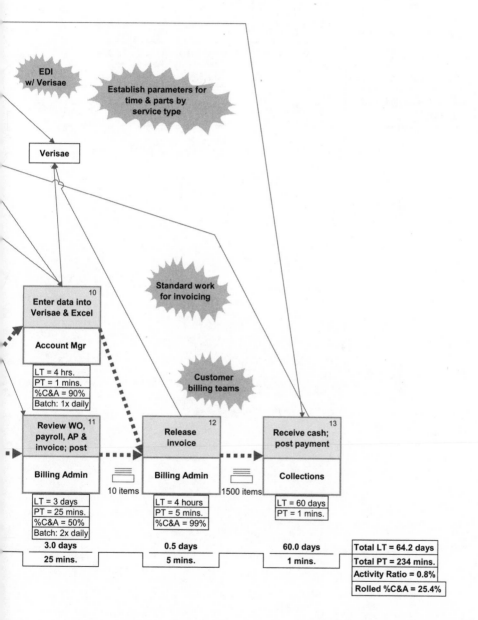

EDI w/ Verisae

Establish parameters for time & parts by service type

Verisae

10
Enter data into Verisae & Excel
Account Mgr
LT = 4 hrs.
PT = 1 mins.
%C&A = 90%
Batch: 1x daily

Standard work for invoicing

Customer billing teams

11
Review WO, payroll, AP & invoice; post
Billing Admin
LT = 3 days
PT = 25 mins.
%C&A = 50%
Batch: 2x daily

10 items

12
Release invoice
Billing Admin
LT = 4 hours
PT = 5 mins.
%C&A = 99%

1500 items

13
Receive cash; post payment
Collections
LT = 60 days
PT = 1 mins.

| 3.0 days | 0.5 days | 60.0 days |
| 25 mins. | 5 mins. | 1 mins. |

Total LT = 64.2 days
Total PT = 234 mins.
Activity Ratio = 0.8%
Rolled %C&A = 25.4%

TABLE D.1   Performance metrics for repair services value stream

Metric	Current State	Projected Future State	Projected % Improvement
Total Lead Time	71.3 days	64.2 days	10.0%
Total Lead Time Excluding Collections	11.3 days	4.2 days	62.8%
Total Process Time	359 minutes	234 minutes	34.8%
Activity Ratio	1.0%	0.8%	-20.0%
Rolled % Complete & Accurate	2.3%	25.4%	1004.4%

APPENDIX E
Shelving Systems Value Stream

The impetus for the value stream mapping activity shown in Figures E.1 and E.2 and Table E.1 was twofold. First, the client wanted to learn what value streams and value stream mapping were all about. While it had been on the Lean journey for several years, it had only experimented with a few of the tactical tools and wanted to explore the fuller benefits that deploying the broader set of Lean principles and practices offered. Second, its competition was starting to deliver higher quality more quickly and at lower cost, and this organization wanted to keep its position as the top shelving supplier.

One of the biggest aha's during current state mapping was the discovery that it had been taking the company an average of 17.5 business days (a little over three weeks!) to generate a quote, which was 23 percent of the total lead time and 29 percent of the quote to final inspection lead time which excludes the billing process.

Note the incredible improvement in Rolled %C&A—from 0.1 percent to 31.6 percent. This is an apt reflection of the power of service level agreements and standard work.

In addition, it was able to eliminate eight hours of non-value-adding hands-on work (process time). While this may not seem significant for a large value stream, given its volumes, this translates into 240,000 freed hours per year, which is the equivalent of 123 FTEs. As the construction industry began to rebound from the recession and the client once again experienced growing demand, this freed capacity reduced the need to increase staffing that would have otherwise been necessary.

FIGURE E.1 Current state value stream map for custom shelving systems

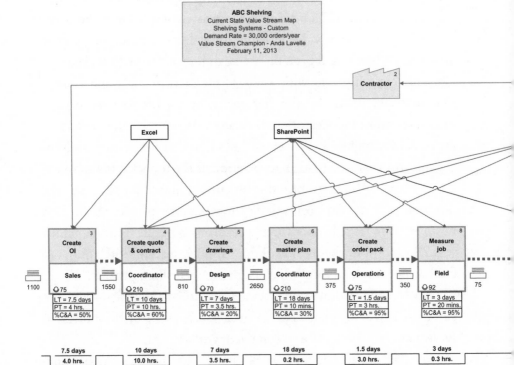

Also, by more fully utilizing its Oracle ERP system, the client was able to discontinue using an application, which saved $250,000 annually in licensing expenses. This type of discovery would likely be missed if the organization had relied solely on process-level mapping.

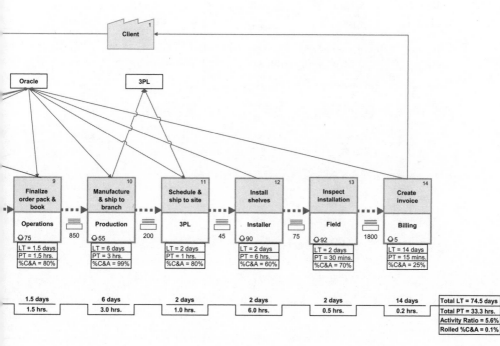

FIGURE E.2 Future state value stream map for custom shelving systems

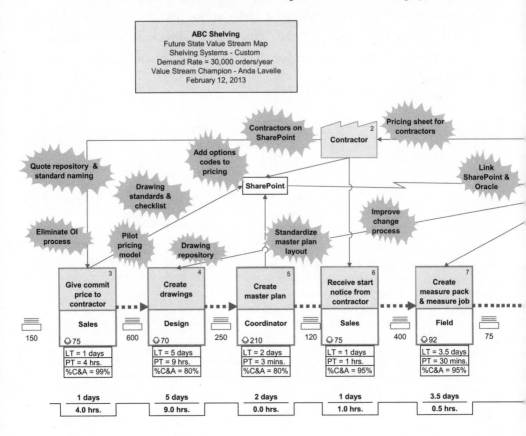

ABC Shelving
Future State Value Stream Map
Shelving Systems - Custom
Demand Rate = 30,000 orders/year
Value Stream Champion - Anda Lavelle
February 12, 2013

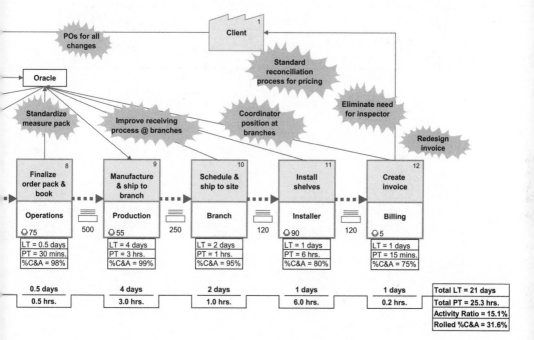

TABLE E.1   Performance metrics for custom shelving systems value stream

Metric	Current State	Projected Future State	Projected % Improvement
Total Lead Time	74.5 days	21 days	71.8%
Total Process Time	33.3 hours	25.3 hours	24.0%
Activity Ratio	5.6%	15.1%	169.6%
Rolled % Complete & Accurate	0.1%	31.6%	31,500.0%

APPENDIX F
Software Development Change Request Value Stream

This example demonstrates the use of value stream mapping to improve a segment of a larger value stream. The value stream mapping activity shown in Figures F.1 and F.2 and Table F.1 was a demonstration project at a software firm that was interested in broadening its Agile development work to include enterprise-wide Lean management practices. The mapping team included the vice president of sales, director of account management, director of operations, marketing manager, director of product management, and two scrum masters.

During the three-day mapping activity, the team had numerous discussions about the role of software testing, customer involvement and responsibility, striking the right balance of iterations, and how "minimal" a minimally viable product should be. Another philosophical discussion centered on redefining how and when sales, account management, and technical teams interfaced directly with the customer. A third major discussion centered on the practice of "grooming" the backlog versus eliminating the backlog.

One of the largest current state discoveries was that the organization had no easy way to track customer requests from order to receipt. As a result, understanding customer demand and the time frames for delivery proved difficult. At the end of the day, three applications used for tracking various parts of the value stream were eliminated and two systems were linked. Now the organization would have fundamental data from which it could measure performance and drive value stream improvement.

As shown on Table F.1, the future state design eliminated almost 30 percent of the hands-on work (process time), and created the abil-

FIGURE F.1 Current state value stream map for software development change request

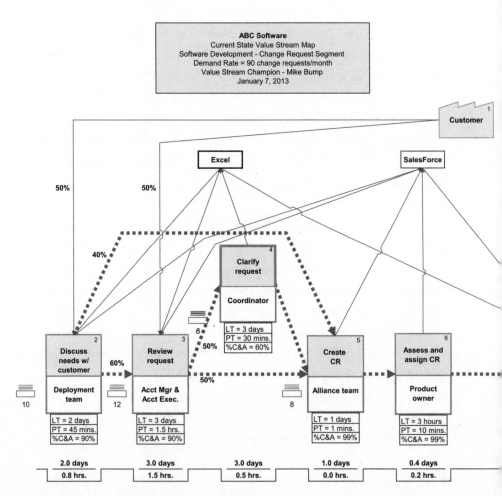

ity for the firm to deliver completed software projects in half the time, with far higher quality and stronger relationships between the functions that make up the value stream.

As with any value stream, there's still more work to be done. This company is currently in stabilization mode and will begin its second round of value stream improvement shortly after this book goes to press.

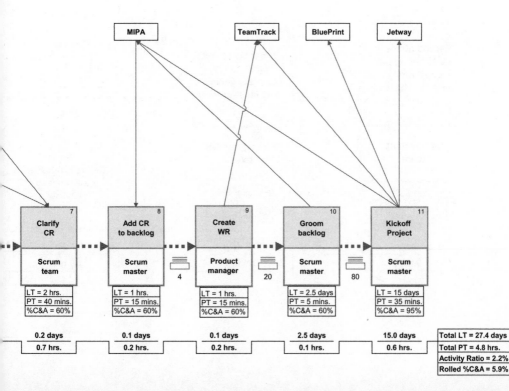

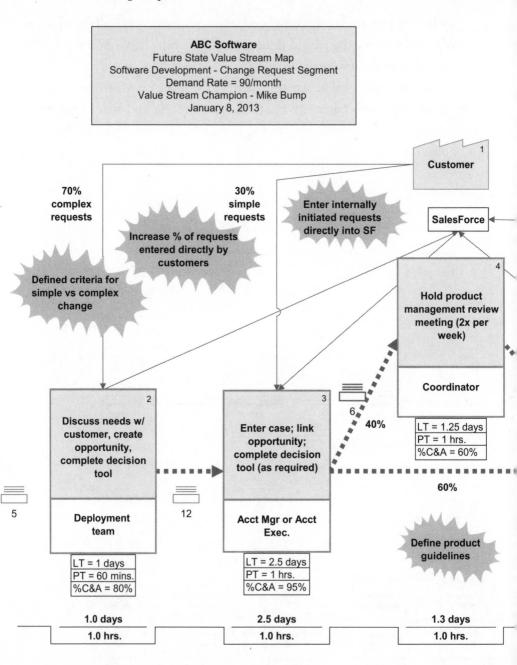

FIGURE F.2 Future state value stream map for software development change request

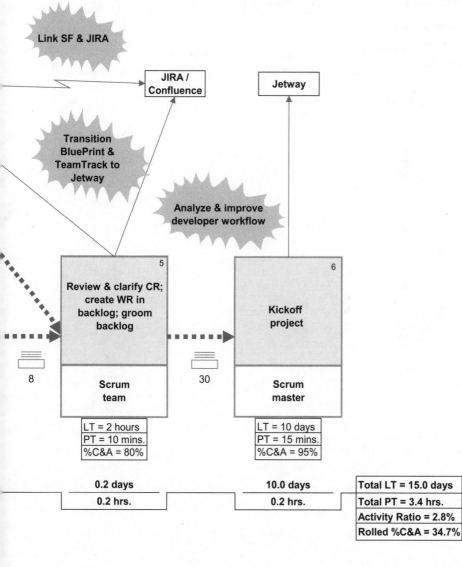

TABLE F.1 Performance metrics for software development change request value stream

Metric	Current State	Projected Future State	Projected % Improvement
Total Lead Time	27.4 days	15.0 days	45.3%
Total Process Time	4.8 hours	3.4 hours	29.2%
Activity Ratio	2.2%	2.8%	27.3%
Rolled % Complete & Accurate	5.9%	34.7%	488.1%

Index

About the Authors

Mike Osterling is the President of Osterling Consulting, Inc., a firm that guides organizations on their Lean journey. With more than 25 years of management experience, Mike has led and supported Lean implementations in the U.S., Mexico, Australia and Europe. He has played a pivotal role in leading Lean transformations across a broad range of industries including manufacturing, construction, engineering, health care, pharmaceuticals, government, military, and oil and gas production. Prior to consulting, Mike played a key role in the Lean transformation at a number of Schneider Electric's facilities.

A founder of San Diego State University's Lean Enterprise Certificate Program, he continues to teach in the program as well as at University of California, San Diego. Mike is fluent in Spanish and is the coauthor of *The Kaizen Event Planner* and *Metrics Based Process Mapping*. He earned his MBA in International Business from San Diego State University and holds a BS in Production and Operations Management. Mike lives in San Diego, California with his wife and two sons and can be contacted through www.mosterling.com.

Karen Martin, President of The Karen Martin Group, has been building, managing, and improving operations for more than 25 years. A leader in applying Lean management practices in non-manufacturing environments, Karen and her team lead Lean transformations and provide business performance improvement support to industry, government agencies, and non-profit organizations.

Karen's background in science (BS in Microbiology, Penn State University and 10 years as a clinical laboratory scientist) and adult learning (MA in Education, California State University, Bakersfield) give her a unique perspective on organizational performance, the improvement process, and achieving results. She receives high marks for her diagnostic skills and ability to rapidly address organizational problems.

Karen is the author of the Shingo Research Award-winning *The Outstanding Organization* and co-author of *Metrics-Based Process Mapping* and *The Kaizen Event Planner*. She teaches at the University of California, San Diego and is an industry advisor for the University of San Diego's Industrial and Systems Engineering program. For more information, please visit www.ksmartin.com.

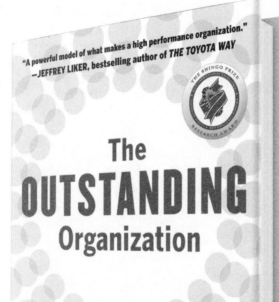